# COSMIC!

## WARWICKSHIRE

Edited by Simon Harwin

First published in Great Britain in 1998 by
*POETRY NOW YOUNG WRITERS*
1-2 Wainman Road, Woodston,
Peterborough, PE2 7BU
Telephone (01733) 230748

All Rights Reserved

*Copyright Contributors 1998*

HB ISBN 0 75430 097 8
SB ISBN 0 75430 098 6

# *FOREWORD*

With over 63,000 entries for this year's Cosmic competition, it has proved to be our most demanding editing year to date.

We were, however, helped immensely by the fantastic standard of entries we received, and, on behalf of the Young Writers team, thank you.

The Cosmic series is a tremendous reflection on the writing abilities of 8-11 year old children, and the teachers who have encouraged them must take a great deal of credit.

We hope that you enjoy reading *Cosmic Warwickshire* and that you are impressed with the variety of poems and style with which they are written, giving an insight into the minds of young children and what they think about the world today.

# CONTENTS

|  |  |
|---|---|
| Gursharon Chagger | 1 |
| **Abbots Farm Junior School** | |
| Hayley Sterne | 1 |
| Heather Cartwright | 2 |
| Kelly Lekeux | 2 |
| Louise Stanley | 3 |
| Rowena Luce | 4 |
| **Allesley Hall Primary School** | |
| Emma Clarke | 4 |
| Sangita Mallick | 5 |
| Rachael-Louise Lawton | 5 |
| Leah Gillon | 6 |
| Joseph Shaw | 6 |
| Matthew Hall | 7 |
| Christopher Fairchild | 7 |
| Natalie White | 8 |
| Haley Shaw | 8 |
| Daniel Jennings | 9 |
| **Bidford-on-Avon CE Primary School** | |
| Matthew Watts | 9 |
| Katie Blundell | 10 |
| Fabia Hully | 10 |
| Samantha Bates | 11 |
| Charlotte Randle | 12 |
| Emma Newman | 12 |
| Sarah Longstaff | 13 |
| Eleanor Tyler | 13 |
| Chris Lawrence | 14 |
| Rebecca Coleman | 14 |
| **Boughton Leigh Junior School** | |
| Naomi Steadman | 15 |

Budbrooke Primary School

| | |
|---|---|
| Stacey Melville | 16 |
| Laura Armstrong | 17 |
| Graham Heydon | 18 |
| Nicholas Calcutt | 19 |
| Matthew Goor | 20 |
| Martina Nicholls | 21 |
| Rachel Goddard | 22 |
| Laura Grantham | 22 |
| Caroline Wilkinson | 23 |
| Rebecca Bradley | 23 |
| Matthew Taylor | 24 |
| Ian Hayes | 24 |
| Lucy Palmer | 25 |
| Matthew Harris | 25 |
| Amy Campbell | 26 |
| Sam Robey | 26 |
| Meghan Lloyd | 27 |
| Ellena Wassall | 27 |
| Cherry Imbush | 28 |
| Simon Wilson | 28 |
| Amy Clarke | 29 |
| David Caine | 29 |
| Emma Dixon | 30 |
| Gareth Davies | 30 |
| Owen Lloyd | 31 |
| Dan Adams | 31 |
| Sammy-Joan Hughes | 32 |
| Stephen Austin | 32 |
| Abi Foster | 33 |

Chetwynd Junior School

| | |
|---|---|
| Michael Rowe | 33 |
| James Leach | 34 |
| Charlotte Spencer | 35 |
| Oliver Manuel | 35 |
| Rachel Axon | 36 |
| Cassandra Rich | 36 |

| | |
|---|---|
| Faith Cosgrove | 37 |
| Ben Hall | 37 |
| Danielle Smith | 38 |
| Rebecca Lane | 38 |
| Leah Thiedeman | 39 |
| Julie Visgandis | 39 |
| Christopher Ayers | 40 |
| Matthew Moore | 40 |
| Chris Johnson | 41 |
| Thomas Leybourne | 41 |
| Daryl Wilkins | 42 |
| Jason Holmes | 42 |
| Tiffany Rae | 43 |
| Richard Thorpe | 43 |
| Debra Lapworth | 44 |

Coughton Primary School

| | |
|---|---|
| Tobie Grovenor-Annis | 44 |
| Victoria Lowe | 45 |
| Rebekah Edwards | 45 |
| Catriona McDonald | 45 |
| Rowena Lewis | 46 |
| Richard Perry | 46 |
| Oliver John Arundel | 47 |
| Jessica Baker | 47 |
| Lauren Jackson | 48 |
| Thomas Zielinski | 48 |
| Felicity Drinkwater | 49 |
| Abigail Turk | 49 |

Crescent School

| | |
|---|---|
| Karina Lickorish | 50 |

Earlsdon Primary School

| | |
|---|---|
| Rachel Arch | 51 |
| Sam Green | 51 |
| Amy Forse | 52 |
| Rajdeep Sandju | 52 |

| | |
|---|---|
| Melissa Holloway | 53 |
| Sarah Davies | 54 |
| Peter Griffin | 54 |
| Georgia Hudson | 55 |
| Alex Bates | 55 |
| Phillippa Harvey | 56 |

Great Alne Primary School

| | |
|---|---|
| Dominic Bostock | 56 |
| Megan Price | 57 |
| Kylie Fowles | 58 |
| Peter Franklin | 59 |
| Kim Lewis | 60 |
| Chloe Steele | 61 |
| Emily Lavender | 62 |
| Carly Alder | 63 |
| Elizabeth Metcalfe | 64 |
| Jayne Lowe | 65 |
| Mariska Wilkins | 66 |
| Victoria Gow | 67 |
| Charlotte Onslow | 68 |
| Gareth Price | 69 |
| Laura Clark | 70 |
| Thomas Smith | 71 |
| Emma Lealan | 72 |
| Becky Stanton | 73 |
| Katie Lamburn | 74 |
| Jennifer Hawkins | 75 |
| Jodie Evans | 76 |

Harbury Primary School

| | |
|---|---|
| Elizabeth Kelly | 76 |
| James Armitage | 77 |
| Thomas Wilkins | 78 |
| Ben Kluth | 78 |
| Alison Shepherd | 79 |
| Elli Bristow | 79 |
| Ashleigh Henry | 80 |

| | |
|---|---|
| Ben Baldwin | 80 |
| Peter Smart | 81 |
| Nadia Bowyer | 81 |
| Alex Corkhill | 82 |
| Katy Grimshaw | 82 |
| James Smart | 83 |
| Megan Nannfeldt | 83 |
| Lee Bettelley | 84 |
| Maria Houghton | 84 |
| Jack Hawkes | 85 |

Ilmington CE Primary School

| | |
|---|---|
| Liz Murray-White | 85 |
| Charlotte Wright | 86 |
| Caitlin Hanrahan | 86 |
| David Griffiths | 87 |
| Lois Stamps | 88 |
| Daisy Blacklock | 89 |
| John Griffiths | 90 |
| Becky Foster | 90 |
| Timothy Smart | 91 |
| Kate Holberton | 91 |
| Hannah Kerby | 92 |
| Peter Griffiths | 92 |
| Jim Sipthorp | 93 |
| Rebecca Brewster | 93 |
| Will Brundle | 94 |
| Athena Pantazievits | 94 |
| Liam Edden | 95 |

Keresley Newland Primary School

| | |
|---|---|
| Emily Hensman | 95 |
| Andrew Wood | 96 |
| Carla MacDonald | 96 |
| Laura Mandara | 97 |
| Faye Randle | 98 |
| Karis Dalziel | 98 |
| Louise Thomas | 99 |

| | |
|---|---|
| Danielle Eddy | 100 |
| Gary Whittle | 101 |

**Mount Nod Primary School**

| | |
|---|---|
| Laura Maton | 101 |
| Ben Tyler | 102 |
| Dean Thomas Wilson | 102 |
| Sam Moore | 102 |
| Peter Green | 103 |
| Stephen Horton | 103 |
| Sammie Fisher | 104 |
| Athena Ashmore | 104 |
| Carly-Ann Bury | 105 |
| Joe Chamberlain | 105 |
| Laura Bass | 106 |
| Hugh Clayden | 106 |
| Kirsty Brooks | 107 |
| Sammy Cossey | 107 |
| Bart Daly | 108 |
| Lois Jones | 108 |
| James Tuck | 109 |
| Amy Clarke | 109 |
| Nicole Lane | 110 |
| Emma Stowe | 110 |

**Nursery Hill Primary School**

| | |
|---|---|
| Katie Tamplin | 111 |
| Leanne Tucker | 111 |
| Leah Moore | 112 |
| Tom Betteridge | 112 |
| Gemma Bradbury | 113 |
| Danielle Radford | 113 |
| Hannah Jones | 114 |
| Greg Shearing | 114 |
| Naomi Beasley | 115 |
| Jack Northall | 115 |
| James Isaacs | 116 |

Race Leys Junior School
- Shelley Hardcastle — 116
- Fern Brown — 117
- Rachel Walker — 117
- Cara Palmer — 118
- Jade Hill — 118
- Rickey Carter — 119
- Josh Neale — 119
- Amy Ann Hill — 120
- Lauren Wayte — 120
- Abigayle Hendry — 121
- Aimee Cotton — 121
- Jenny Marshall — 122

St Anne's RC Primary School, Nuneaton
- Ian Gough — 123
- Ashley Mears — 123
- Craig Sweeney — 124
- Jamie Wyatt — 124

St Faith's CE Junior School, Alcester
- Gemma Pamment — 125
- Becky Chester — 125
- Jennifer Howes — 126
- Hannah Muitt — 126
- Jessica Harrison — 127
- Naomi Blayney — 127
- Christine Wilkinson — 128
- Anne Gould-Fellows — 128
- Olivia Beeson — 129
- Penelope Sarah Eileen Mills — 130
- Claire Wood — 131
- Sarah Grant — 132
- Sophie A Merrick — 133
- Louise Foy — 134
- Harriet Bradley — 135

St Matthew's Bloxam CE Primary School, Rugby
- Ian Maguire — 136
- Reena Tank — 136
- Emillie Jones-Cutter — 137
- Rita Chauhan — 137
- Aysha Khurshid — 138
- Jayna Mistry — 138
- Nathan Woolery — 139
- Scarlett F L G Chamberlain — 139
- Katie Morse — 140
- Hayley McGowan — 140
- Andrew Miles — 141
- Katie Beattie — 141
- David Simpson — 142
- Daniel Gelston — 143
- Priya Mistry — 144

St Peter's CE Primary School, Nuneaton
- Melissa Forman — 144
- Elizabeth Morton — 145
- Jenny Mepham — 146
- Sophie Sutton — 147
- Emily Brooke — 148
- Felicity Sargent — 149
- Natalie Horton — 150
- Laura Teece — 151
- Rowenna Chartres — 152
- Felicity Melia — 152
- Wayne Saunders — 153
- Verity Hatfield — 153
- Nick Vennart — 154
- Kyan Cheng — 154
- Tom Kelly — 155
- Luke Bonser — 155
- Meg Donaldson — 156
- Rebecca Boston — 156
- Rachel Cardani — 157
- Matthew Goodwin — 157

Stivichall Primary School
- Melanie James — 158
- Simon Parsons — 158
- Sophie Meakin — 159
- Hannah Woodcock — 159
- Samantha Bolus — 160
- Gemma Brown — 160
- Elliot Batchelor — 161
- Jamie Reinwalt — 161
- Hannah Greyson-Gaito — 162
- Suneil Jaspal — 162
- Matthew Mullen — 163
- Lauren Byrne — 163
- Kirstie Simpson — 164
- Sam Strumidlo — 164
- Tom Price — 165
- Ketna Mistry — 165
- Kimberley Jones — 166
- Jessica McGarry — 166
- Ryan Waite — 167

Stratford Preparatory School
- Elliot Krauze — 167
- Abigail Tompkins — 168
- Charles Hewitt — 168
- Emma Hogg — 169
- Kelly Gregg — 170
- Clementine Hutsby — 170
- Hannah Pashley — 171
- Rupert Daffern — 171
- Olivia Newton — 172
- Edward Hogg — 172
- Emma Hunt — 173
- Kate Wells — 173
- Sarah Harris — 174
- Edward Collins — 174
- Ross McDermott — 175
- Sophie Roberts — 176

| | | |
|---|---|---|
| | Jaryd Buggins | 176 |
| **The Croft School** | | |
| | Nishath Hussain | 177 |
| **Tysoe CE Primary School** | | |
| | Eleanor Collins | 178 |
| | Stuart Prickett | 178 |
| | Rachael Nilsson | 179 |
| | Rhian Melton | 179 |
| | Corrin Ascott | 180 |
| | Ashley Guest | 180 |
| | Emily Sayer | 181 |
| | Nancy Day | 181 |
| | Jessica Sayer | 182 |
| | Gareth Cotter | 182 |
| | Katie Luckett | 183 |
| **Wellesbourne Primary School** | | |
| | Nicola Davison | 183 |
| | Toni Dobson | 184 |
| | Roxanne Cooknell | 185 |
| | Jade Brain | 185 |
| | Adam Payne | 186 |
| | Adam Trinder | 186 |
| | Emily Woods | 186 |
| | Tom Essex | 187 |
| | Ben Elliott | 187 |
| | Lindsey Marie Fullwood | 187 |
| | Charlotte Schofield | 188 |
| | Carrie Alford | 188 |
| | Laura McEveney | 188 |
| | Chris Waddoups | 189 |
| | Elizabeth Kyriakopoulou | 189 |
| | Daniel Kettle | 189 |
| | Chris Brindle | 190 |
| | Callam Green | 190 |
| | Graham Shone | 191 |

| | |
|---|---|
| Louise Fawcett | 191 |
| Ashleigh Piotrowski | 192 |
| Kylee Smith | 192 |
| Sophie Tilley | 193 |

Whitley Abbey Primary School

| | |
|---|---|
| Amardeep S Thandi | 193 |
| Steven Woodward | 194 |
| Martin Hawkes | 194 |
| Tara McEnery | 195 |
| Donna Ann Thacker | 195 |
| Esther Sewell | 196 |
| Karly Jayne Bedding | 196 |
| Gemma Louise | 197 |
| Kirsty Browett | 198 |
| Nicola J Clark | 199 |

# THE POEMS

## WATER

Drip drop drip drop,
Down the window-pane
Like snakes.
Splish Splash rushing down,
Falling in large puddles.
Splash Splash.
Ripples bubbles,
Of sparkling drops.
Reflections swirling down.

*Gursharon Chagger (10)*


## ELIZABETH I

Elizabeth the First
Wasn't so kind
She hacked people's heads off
In double-quick time.

She was very pale
She looked very weak
Don't ask her to smile
'Cos she's got big black teeth.

Was she pushed or did she fall?
Well nobody knows for sure.

She didn't lose her head
But now she's long dead
Perhaps she still walks and
Whispers and talks
In the corridors of long long ago.

*Hayley Sterne (10)*
*Abbots Farm Junior School*

## NOSES

My dad's nose has a mind of its own
It sniffs and sniffs all day long.
When Dad gets a cold it has great fun,
Because his nose likes to run.
My dad squeezes it with a handkerchief,
Because . . . I'll make it brief,
Dad tries to suffocate it,
Because he doesn't like it one bit.
My mum's nose is always red,
So we put it straight to bed.
When Mum's got a cold, it dances
And it holds up her glasses.
A hooter is a funny thing,
And when you sniff, it makes a din.
My brother's nose is different,
It's long and big and quite bent.
All he does is sniff it up,
Just like a powerful jump.
His nose is fairly snotty and hairy.
My nose is always blocked
Right the way around the clock.

*Heather Cartwright (10)*
*Abbots Farm Junior School*


## HALLOWE'EN

It's Hallowe'en, it's Hallowe'en
When ghosts rise from the dead
Witches come from other lands
To chop of people's heads.

It's Hallowe'en, it's Hallowe'en
When ghosts come through locked doors
Through wardrobes, ceilings anywhere
Sometimes through the floors.

It's Hallowe'en, it's Hallowe'en
When corpses rise from the dead
They haunt children in their dreams
When they're safely tucked in bed.

It's Hallowe'en, it's Hallowe'en
It's time to celebrate
Trick or treating's fun to do
I think Hallowe'en's great.

*Kelly Lekeux (10)*
*Abbots Farm Junior School*


## THE TOWN'S HEDGEHOG

The town has a hedgehog
Although it's never spoken to me,
It has a very nice little friend -
Called but a sweet buzzy bee.

The hedgehog's name is JE5OT
How good does that sound to you?
It sounds like a funny calm name -
I hope you think so too.

Thinking about it to meet this fellow
You'd need to ride down on the coast,
And listen for his friend playing the cello
Just maybe they'll invite you in for a slice of toast.

So now I tell you
Doesn't it sound worthwhile,
Take a trip, don't except a whip.
And you'll find yourself -
That I can't tell!

*Louise Stanley (10)*
*Abbots Farm Junior School*

## SUMMER

Summer is a lovely and warm time of year.
Flowers will come and the birds will live.
The trees will grow and touch the sky.
The birds will sing with their joy.
We will sunbathe and turn a crispy gold.
Living things will spread their joy for
The summer God has arrived.

*Rowena Luce (10)*
*Abbots Farm Junior School*


## THE SCHOOL-DAY

Ten to nine the whistle blows
All stand still then all make rows
Into the classroom we all march
Do not push, do not charge
To our tables we must go
Not too fast, not too slow
Out come books, out come pens
Working hard till half-past ten
Playtime's over far too quick
Back inside quick, quick, quick
Work till twelve then dinner comes
Line up nicely to fill our tums
It's ten past one dinner's over
Back to class to start all over
Soon the clock says half-past three
Run to the gate and home for tea.

*Emma Clarke (9)*
*Allesley Hall Primary School*

## LEO THE LION

Leo is a fierce lion,
His favourite meal is deer.
Leo sneaks up on the grass
Ready to catch his prey:
He snarls and then . . . pounces,
Grabbing the poor, harmless animal,
Tearing it to bits with his almighty teeth:
Leo is a fierce lion.
Leo is a golden, gentle lion,
His fur and mane are shining bright.
He has sharp eyes to watch and scare his prey;
Leo has a wife and two babies and he loves
them very much,
He knows when his babies are in trouble and
when they are not:
Leo is a golden, gentle lion.
Leo is a clever lion,
He is very furry with his golden fur.
Leo is a frightening lion when he raises his hackles,
Leo is a clever lion.

*Sangita Mallick (7)*
*Allesley Hall Primary School*


## DOLPHINS

I love to swim in the ocean
Deep and wide.
I like to swim with dolphins that
Make me smile.
They love me and I love them
We play together day and night.

*Rachael-Louise Lawton (7)*
*Allesley Hall Primary School*

## A Rat's Life

You roam the streets of London
looking for a nice big bin,
all you want to do is find some food
and nobody seems to care,
They spot you and they call
*The rat man!*
You and your mates
shudder and flee
for your lives when you hear that name
but nobody seems to care,
Nobody seems to care
what you go through,
You haven't a friend
in the world
you're just a
lonely rat.

*Leah Gillon (11)*
*Allesley Hall Primary School*

## My Dog Beau

My dog Beau runs about upstairs downstairs
She even goes out.
She gets her stick and gives it to me
She wants me to play, no way José!
She comes upstairs and into my bed
She doesn't play but goes to sleep instead.

*Joseph Shaw (8)*
*Allesley Hall Primary School*

## FOOTBALL

I am football mad.
My brother is sad,
'Cos City are losing,
Huckerby hit the post,
Dublin hit the bar,
Strachan's eyes are twinkling like a star.

Man U are one up,
All we can hope for is a draw.
Naughty Van Der Gouw,
He kicked Telfer on the head,
His head is sore.
We lost the game never mind.
There is just no goal to find.

*Matthew Hall (8)*
*Allesley Hall Primary School*

## HUNTING AND FISHING

Hunting and fishing are bad it makes me sad.
Most people hunt with a gun they say it is fun.
Some people fish with a rod they kill fish like
Salmon and cod.
Most fishermen take the fish to sell
They tell you to buy the fish.
Some hunters hunt deer.
Cavemen hunted with a spear.

*Christopher Fairchild (8)*
*Allesley Hall Primary School*

## IN THE DUSTY STREET

In the dusty street
Traffic rumbles
Fumes rage
Cats purr on walls
Ladies with prams
Babies crying
Dogs barking
Litter everywhere
Dusty floors
Hedge being cut
People talking
Children playing
That's what the dusty street is like.

*Natalie White (9)*
*Allesley Hall Primary School*


## MORAG THE WEARY COW

Morag how do you feel
I hear nothing
I watch the weary cow every day
eating in the same old spot
until there is nothing there
boys come every day
they call her names throw stones
but still the weary old cow lives on.

*Haley Shaw (11)*
*Allesley Hall Primary School*

### SPIKE IN TOWN

Good, great Spike,
trampling through mud,
making cars and houses muddy,
chasing after cats,
upsetting happy babies,
escaping dog catchers,
eating scraps from tramps,
waking people up in the mornings,
you betray no resentment,
you definitely deserve more.

*Daniel Jennings (10)*
*Allesley Hall Primary School*


## WORMS

W is for worm
Squirmy worms
Furry worms
Or ones with little green socks
You better not mock
Or they will attack in flocks
To turn you into a squirmy pink worm!

But would they dare
Dangle from your hair
In a mince meat factory
Or slither in Mrs Blither's kitchen
Amongst paste and spread
And have a head to head with tomorrow's dinner?

*Matthew Watts (11)*
*Bidford-on-Avon CE Primary School*

## THE WAY TO BETHLEHEM

People plodding on the road,
Hot exhausting sun,
People panting thirsting for drinks,
but the knobbly pebbled roads don't seem to stop,
Tiring people begin to slow,
Desert sands burn,
The beautiful sunset glows in the sky,
Pots, pans and other things hit the donkeys,
Then they see a town,
Is it Bethlehem they wonder,
They go around Bethlehem to find a place to stay,
Then a nice man says 'I have no room here but I have a stable'
They walk into the stable and they lay in the cosy hay.

*Katie Blundell (11)*
*Bidford-on-Avon CE Primary School*


## CURLY WORMS

Curly worms
Wiggle and squirm
Silently they swirl
Slimily they curl

Long worms, thin worms
Short worms, fat worms
Slow creatures in the soil
Useful toil

They don't need eyes to see in the dark
They would burrow down deep if a dog should bark
All our very best wishes we send
To the worm, the gardener's friend.

*Fabia Hully (10)*
***Bidford-on-Avon CE Primary School***

## SPRING

It's the end of the hibernation,
Animals are awakening from a deep sleep,
Birds are chirping.
Everything is coming back to life,
There is a breath of wind,
Rabbits hopping around the fields,
Nuzzling foals annoying their dads,
Newborn lambs suckling on their mothers,
First of the blossom is arriving,
Banks of primroses are everywhere,
A busy shepherd is counting the sheep,
And newborn lambs are running around,
A clutch of eggs are in Mrs Brown's basket,
Soaring skylarks are playing in the sky,
Chattering sparrows on the fence,
Swans and their cygnets in the lake
Gathering frogspawn in the pond,
Leaping salmon in the river,
There is a clear blue sky,
Only a couple of clouds,
I wish it was always springtime.

*Samantha Bates (11)*
***Bidford-on-Avon CE Primary School***

## BABY JESUS

As you walk in the stable the hay scratches your legs
The breath of the animals fills the room
Noisy people outside talking about
where they are going to stay for the night
In the night baby Jesus is born,
with his soft skin against Mary's
Doves cooing as baby Jesus cries,
in Mary's arms pulling funny faces
Mary laughing with happiness
Animals looking in amazement
Baby Jesus snuggles up warmly in the hay
And falls asleep in the hay.

*Charlotte Randle (10)*
*Bidford-on-Avon CE Primary School*




## THE BRIGHT STAR

Darkness submerges the fiery sunset
Stars illuminate the midnight sky
The moon casts an eerie light
One bright star is standing proud
Looking down from its dark home
Signifying a king is born
All stars bow to admire its splendour
In the dark mass of night.

*Emma Newman (11)*
*Bidford-on-Avon CE Primary School*

## Rubbish

I looked in a book on rubbish,
When suddenly I got sucked in,
I wondered what the smell was,
I realised I was in the bin,
All I could smell was rotten food,
It was so disgusting,
And ever so rude,
It was really really yucky when I had a look,
So I ran straight to the end of the book,
I suddenly popped out,
I was in the library once again,
I could smell the lovely polish,
Now I knew enough on rubbish to do my homework.

*Sarah Longstaff (10)*
*Bidford-on-Avon CE Primary School*


## The Star

The silky sky uncovers the stars
Glittering, shining in the never ending black
For they twinkle and shimmer.
Moonlit paths winding down the road
While one new glorious bright star
Takes its place in the great sheet above us
Showing our saviour Jesus Christ.

*Eleanor Tyler (10)*
*Bidford-on-Avon CE Primary School*

## THE STAR

The bright star shone in the midnight sky
Hovering over the town of Bethlehem
Shining stars surrounded it
As they danced into the darkness
The dark quilt of night encircling them
As they twinkled in the moonlight
But the brightest star of all
Stood high above a stable
A stable where a baby slept
Soon to be king of Earth.

*Chris Lawrence (10)*
*Bidford-on-Avon CE Primary School*


## WINTER

Little winding paths covered by sheets of snow
Lifeless trees stripped of their leaves
Icicles like crystals hang off the trees
Sheep huddled together shivering with cold
Glowing snowflakes fall from the pure white sky
Thin ice covers streams
Gold autumn leaves vanish under white sheets of snow
Featureless landscape
Arctic conditions.

*Rebecca Coleman (11)*
*Bidford-on-Avon CE Primary School*

## WHY ME?

'Tidy your room Naomi.'
My mum said to me,
My reply was
'Why me?'

She gives me a list of reasons,
Why I should tidy my room.
I say 'Iona made half the mess
'cause she has half the room.'

'Tidy your room Naomi.'
My mum said to me,
My reply was
'Why me?'

I go have a little look
And see the mess that's there.
(Gasp) It looks like a bomb's hit it!
*There*! And *There!* And *There!*

'Tidy your room Naomi.'
My mum said to me,
My reply was
'Why me?'

But now I see the reason why
I should tidy up.
All the teddies and the crayons
I am a messy pup.

'Tidy your room Naomi.'
My mum said to me,
'OK, Mum. But . . .
Why me?'

*Naomi Steadman (9)*
***Boughton Leigh Junior School***

## PACIFIC 231

Stomping, rumbling movements
The rotten old pistons thud.
Frantic puffs of steam start whooshing up
From the train.
The stationmaster signals the train,
Children wave while the train picks up speed
And movement comes.
A man sees meadows of green flowers on hills,
A tramp on the side watching the glee people
While haven't a shilling on his blanket
Trying to play his harmonica in the freezing cold.
Rivers and streams whirling round and under bridges.
Combine harvesters chewing up grain and wheat.
Bolting, jolting, speedily under tunnels,
While men on way to work on their toddle.
Joyfully they smile at the train driver.
Booming, banging, chomping cogs,
Rapidly stopping for next Marylebone Station.
Whooping dog-eared chugging noises while train judders,
People then jump for doors . . .

*Stacey Melville (11)*
*Budbrooke Primary School*

## IN THE GARDEN OF WINTER

In the garden of winter,
One fluffy squirrel nibbles some nuts,

In the garden of winter,
Two plump robins perch in a tree,

In the garden of winter,
Three white snowdrops burst up from the ground,

In the garden of winter,
Four shivering mice shelter from the frosty wind,

In the garden of winter,
Five wavy trees lose their summer coats,

In the garden of winter,
Six hairy spiders cling to their frosty webs,

In the garden of winter,
Seven tiny sparrows twitter in the treetops,

In the garden of winter,
Eight sparkling snowflakes flutter to the ground.

*Laura Armstrong (10)*
*Budbrooke Primary School*

## DUEL OF THE EAGLES!

Spitfires take the air,
Breathtaking moments for the
Teenagers with no experience,
Fearsome fighting of eagles,
Edge of the seat stuff.
Zooming around like a roller-coaster,
Through the candyfloss,
Spitfires biting chunks out of the 109s
Like an eagle would its prey,
Speeding like a lightning bolt.
Diving, dipping, swerving, dunking,
Seeping, plunging,
I was scared stiff.
I was hysterically looking for 109s
Red one be . . .
Oil everywhere
Scolding temperature
I escaped.
*No.*
My *parach* . . .
One life wasted in one split second.

**Graham Heydon (10)**
**Budbrooke Primary School**

## IN THE GARDEN OF WINTER

In the garden of winter,
One sparkling snowflake
Falls on the dewy ground.

In the garden of winter,
Two children make a lonely
Snowman elegant and round.

In the garden of winter,
Three squirrels pounce around
On the leaves of the trees.

In the garden of winter,
Four sparrows flap around
The window.

In the garden of winter,
Five lost golden leaves
Swiftly dance off the last few trees.

In the garden of winter,
Six mice squeak to find a warm
Hiding place for the rest of the
                            *winter!*

***Nicholas Calcutt (11)***
***Budbrooke Primary School***

## IN THE STREETS OF WINTER ...

In the streets of winter a house gains
its white fleece,
In the streets of winter two trees receive
their white flakes,
In the streets of winter three children
troop off to fetch their Christmas cakes,
In the streets of winter four carol singers
singing Christmas tunes,
In the streets of winter five children
enjoying the snow,
In the streets of winter six children
with a cold,
In the streets of winter seven cars
that won't start,
In the streets of winter eight Christians
walking back from church,
In the streets of winter nine red robins
stood on the snow coated grass,
In the streets of winter ten Christmas
trees being delivered,
In the streets of winter is the sound
of twelve households fast asleep.

*Matthew Goor (11)*
*Budbrooke Primary School*

## IN THE GARDENS IN WINTER

In the gardens in winter,
One lonely robin shelters on a plant pot.

In the gardens in winter,
Two excited children play with the
freezing, icy snow.

In the gardens in winter,
Three tiny, delicate white snowdrops
Whistle in the biting wind.

In the gardens in winter,
Four bare, naked trees shatter furiously.

In the gardens in winter,
Five chirping blackbirds singing
For spring.

In the gardens in winter,
Six blades of grass poking through
The soft, fleecy blanket of snow.

In the gardens in winter,
Seven glistening icicles hanging
From the ice-attacked frosted roof.

*Martina Nicholls (11)*
*Budbrooke Primary School*

## PACIFIC 231

Giant steam train rumbling round and round inside,
Hot and fiery warm inside,
Asleep in a nice warm shed,
'Peep' time to get out of bed,
Nice and warm inside and wide awake,
Rumbling, roaring, raring to go,
Mighty as can be, he still starts slow,
Steadily going along the track,
Faster and faster, racing like the wind,
Galloping like a horse,
As fast as a thunder bolt,
Up hills and along rivers,
Soaring like a bird on a track,
Journey's end is just in view,
Slower and slower, smelly and sleepy
Slow and sleepy after a long journey he halts
Giving a screech like a bird,
A hard day's work he goes to bed
To sleep for another day.

*Rachel Goddard (11)*
*Budbrooke Primary School*


## BALLOONS

Balloons always flying
Always in the air
Look up in the sky
Look there's a balloon
Oh it's so beautiful
On the blue sky
Now I wish I could fly
Soon in a balloon.

*Laura Grantham (8)*
*Budbrooke Primary School*

## PACIFIC 231

Sleeping, waiting, like a massive lion waiting
to pounce on its prey.
Its lumbering, heavy-tuned engine sleeping at
the foot of the journey.
Slowly it wakes up to a jerky start,
Pacing to and fro, steam pouring up and out,
The lion jumps from its bed and begins its journey.

Rivers and streams go hurtling by,
Faster and faster in the blink of an eye.
Meadows, sweet lambs and rams, all gone
completely in less than a glimpse,
Swiftly it sprints along the way,
Smoky, hilly, that firing rain.
'Come on, come on we're nearly there,' chugs the train.
'I mustn't stop now, I say now we're there!'
A sudden halt becomes slow, lower and lower
The steam becomes no longer to blow!

*Caroline Wilkinson (11)*
*Budbrooke Primary School*


## BUTTERFLY

B  eautiful flying
U  p in the air
T  earing through the sky
T  ill there's no daylight
E  very night you're swooping
R  iding in your flight
F  lying to your nest
L  ying down to rest
Y  ou are now asleep.

*Rebecca Bradley (8)*
*Budbrooke Primary School*

## PACIFIC 231

The metallic lumbering giant moves his drowsy eyes,
As if he has just woke from eternal slumber,
His pistons start to heave and ho
As if a yawn may be heard,
His pistons use all their might,
Its huge ginormous bulk forces it to the track,
Wind will pelt against its shimmering body,
As if it was to shatter there and then,
People see glimpses of marshy meadows,
Shallowing sheep, field and fences all nice and neat,
Withering plants, bridges and buildings
And rigid rivers, as it sprints along,
Its wheels are bolting as if to say
I can't take it anymore,
It's hurtling faster and faster,
Suddenly a sound of thunder as the
231 comes to a halt.

*Matthew Taylor (11)*
*Budbrooke Primary School*


## AEROPLANE

A lready up in the air
E nchanting the sky
R iding the wind
O n top of the clouds
P assing over the trees
L ooping and swooping
A n experience
N ever imagined
E nding soon.

*Ian Hayes (8)*
*Budbrooke Primary School*

## TERROR

Terror
Blood-red eyes glaring in rage
Terror
Chains rattling, desperately trying to break free
Terror
Floorboards creaking, getting closer and closer
Terror
A werewolf howling faintly but frighteningly
Terror
Pictures watching you, staring with fright
Terror
Black cats watching, foggy fields and ditches
Old broomsticks that look as if they're witches
Not a speck of light just a thick cloak of black
*Terror.*

***Lucy Palmer (10)***
***Budbrooke Primary School***


## AEROPLANES

A  eroplanes up in the sky,
E  agle eye views,
R  ed Arrows oh my,
O  rvil and Wright were first to crew,
P  ropellers ready here we go.
L  ancasters oh no!
A  eroplanes high and low,
N  o waiting here we go.
E  ck!

***Matthew Harris (8)***
***Budbrooke Primary School***

## PACIFIC 231

There I sat as still as a stone, waiting, waiting.
I felt my pistons turn my wheels and force me to
gradually go forth,
As I was an enormous metallic animal
I had to pull hundreds of stubborn carriages,
So I pulled the never ending string of them on and on,
Soon fields and fences, hedges and hawthorn, bushes
and birds were whizzing by in a blurry picture,
Off I went rising and falling, rushing and
racing over the hills,
I felt the dawn wind brush my face
as I jerked to a halt,
At last I can again sit as still as a stone,
waiting, waiting.

*Amy Campbell (10)*
*Budbrooke Primary School*


## AEROPLANES

A eroplanes fly through the air.
E ngines burn off fuel.
R ocket engines showing their fire.
O f course we never forget the Wrights.
P lanes whizzing to and fro.
L ightly drifting through the air.
A fighter comes rocketing through the sky.
N ever giving up on a journey.
E xactly pin-pointed by the control tower.

*Sam Robey (8)*
*Budbrooke Primary School*

## PACIFIC 231
*(Inspired by the music Pacific 231 by Honegger)*

People anxiously waiting for their train to approach
It's Pacific 231 which has 35 coaches
With a blow from a whistle the train
Whisks away running smoothly along the railway
Past rivers, lakes, meadows and fields
The 231 clanks its wheels
The smell of its smoke fills the air
The metallic lumbering giant reaches station 11
Past neat lines of daisies a tramp on a bench
The 231 reaches journey's end
With a slow down of its engine and
A toot of its horn the 231 runs
No more!

*Meghan Lloyd (11)*
*Budbrooke Primary School*



## AEROPLANE

A n aeroplane flying high.
E very day up in the sky,
R ed Arrows are a type of plane,
O ver the clouds up, up and away,
P iper tiny but still can fly,
L indenberg a famous man for his flight.
A nyone can ride in them,
N ow you know, enjoy
E very flight.

*Ellena Wassall (8)*
*Budbrooke Primary School*

## A Night In Ghost House

A snowy owl hoots noisily and spookily up in the high branches
in the cold outside.
Creak, creak the heavy, stiff, rusty, oak door bolt turns making the
dust shake.
The creaky heavy oak door opens
making the creaking squeaking noise.
The grandfather clock starts clicking constantly ticking at
a steady rhythm.
The clanging clock chimes. Ding! Ding! Ding! Ding!
Strikes 4 o'clock in the morning.
The squeaky footsteps of the platformed boots clonking,
Thudding and thumping heavily
making the unbalanced floorboards squeak under every step.
The screeching piercing noise of the high-pitched laughter burst out.

*Cherry Imbush (10)*
*Budbrooke Primary School*


## Aeroplanes

A eroplanes flying in the sky,
E ven little ones fly very high.
R iding through a fluffy cloud,
O n the engine it would be loud.
P ropellers going round and round,
L isten to that noisy sound.
A nd down and down we go,
N ow we are very low.
E xactly going down to land,
S o that ride was grand.

*Simon Wilson (8)*
*Budbrooke Primary School*

## KINGFISHER

A streak of blue under the sky,
A sparkling flash of lightning,
A breast of fire, a crest of gold,
Ruby wings and jet-black eyes,
He skims over the water,
He flies over the valley,
In the blink of an eye he's seized a fish,
Taking it home to his family,
He wears a velvet cloak of sapphires and emeralds,
His song is as sweet as honey,
His appearance is so sleek,
My blessing will always be
On the fiery kingfisher's beak.

*Amy Clarke (10)*
*Budbrooke Primary School*


## LAUGHTER AT FOUR

A tawny owl hoots from the wood.
A door's metallic bolt echoes clear and loud.
The door swings open with a groan.
The wind whooshes and howls.
A wooden floorboard creeks.
The clock ticks and tocks noisily.
Steps shuffle and clump along.
The clock chimes four thunderously.
Cackling of laughter of a murderer at work.
The door booms boisterously shut.

*David Caine (10)*
*Budbrooke Primary School*

## PACIFIC 231

Huge and heavy steam train was 300 tonnes.
Powerful mighty engine
People putting coal into the fire making the steam engine go.
Rumbling raring to go slowly but getting faster and faster.
Speeding up quite well now.
Passing loads of meadows with galloping like a horse in smelly and ponging pigs.
By this time we are racing like the wind.
Going up and down in and out.
The engine was hot, boiling, fiery.
Tired and sleepy ready to slow down coming to a halt.
Time for another night sleep.

*Emma Dixon (10)*
*Budbrooke Primary School*


## HELICOPTERS

H igh rotors are spinning
E ver so fast
L nyx the Army helicopter
I climb in ready to fly
C oping with the noise
O ff we go
P ictures from the sky
T earing through the sky
E agle we see
R eady to land.

*Gareth Davies (8)*
*Budbrooke Primary School*

## FLYING FISH

F lying fish
L eaping out of the water
Y ou can see them go
I n the air
N owt they said to me
G lowing eyes under water

F lying down again
I wish I was one
S ometimes don't you
H ow I would like to be one
              Don't you?

*Owen Lloyd (8)*
*Budbrooke Primary School*


## A WALK THROUGH THE ENCHANTED HOUSE

The owl hoots wildly from the woods
The rusty bolt opens stiffly
The creaking of the heavy oak door
The old grandfather clock ticks in its usual rhythm
Tick! Tock! Tick! Tock!
Heavy thudding noisily along the landing.
Creaky floorboards creak creepily.
The noisy clock blares out its early morning chime.
The ghosts and ghouls laugh deafeningly at their
uninvited guests.
The old oak door slams thunderously shut!

*Dan Adams (10)*
*Budbrooke Primary School*

## BUTTERFLIES

B utterflies butterflies
U nusual as they are
T rouble sometimes
T rouble always!
E verywhere they fly
R ed, green, orange, yellow, pink and blue
F luttering everywhere.
L ively colours everywhere
I t's very very very pretty
E ven though it is just an insect
S o happy they make me.

*Sammy-Joan Hughes (8)*
*Budbrooke Primary School*


## HORROR IN THE DARK

The hoot of the owl hooting away.
Slowly the floor starts to creak from very
loud footsteps.
The sound of the old oak door
That starts to make a racket.
And evil clank of the locks and
Bolts then suddenly silence . . .
Ha ha ha ha ha -
Then the shriek of a lady screaming for help -
Then suddenly the start of noises . . .
The grandfather clock starts to ding.

*Stephen Austin (11)*
*Budbrooke Primary School*

## ON A HEDGE IN WINTER

On a hedge in winter, one lonely blackbird pecks at the berries.
On a hedge in winter, two mice leap out in search for food.
On a hedge in winter, three twigs snap and fall.
On a hedge in winter, four robins meet and chat.
On a hedge in winter, five berries freeze and curl.
On a hedge in winter, six drops of delicate snow settles and fades.
On a hedge in winter, seven crushed wrappers rustle by.
On a hedge in winter, eight snowballs go skidding past.
On a hedge in winter, nine geese come honking over.
On a hedge in winter, ten people stare,
At the frozen old scared hedgerow that's now looking rather bare.

*Abi Foster (10)*
*Budbrooke Primary School*


## NUNEATON

Nuneaton, hundreds of people,
All trying to do their shopping.
Toy shops, food shops
Clothes shops, hundreds of shops.

The many roads busy with noisy people.
Hustle and bustle at the market.
The sounds of children pleading for toys,
Cries from the market sellers
Advertising their trade,
People laughing and talking.

Nuneaton?
Okay so it's drab and dreary,
But people shop there
So it can't be that bad.

*Michael Rowe (10)*
*Chetwynd Junior School*

## MY DOG REBEL

My dog Rebel
Played and played with me and my brother.
We played football, fetch and racing.
*Wait!*
But he was a little naughty.
When I woke up in the morning,
I went downstairs and woke him up
And he carried on with the plan.
*Wait!*
'Woof! Woof!' he barked.
'Mum!' brother cried,
'Dad!' Mum screamed,
'Good morning' said Dad.
*Wait!*
I live at number thirteen,
I did live at number four,
He just might be dead now,
But I still love him, wherever he is.
*Wait!*
His ball is in my attic,
And my cart that I used to give him a ride in.
His stick is broken in half,
And he's gone.
He won every race he joined in.
He was called Rebel
Because he liked Star Wars!
      *Wait!*

***James Leach (8)***
***Chetwynd Junior School***

## Rain

A blanket of raindrops,
Spitting at the floor,
Clattering against the concrete,
Wrestling with each other.

The rain swimming along,
Waiting to get to the drizzle club.
Where it can eat spitburgers
And play slipball.

The wind singing with
The angels, while they lightly
Float across the jungle
Of growling clouds below.

The trees are swaying,
To the sound of the music,
With their branches
Dancing in the wind.

*Charlotte Spencer (11)*
*Chetwynd Junior School*


## The Raging Weather

The dingy, grey clouds,
like the colour of a pencil lead, hovering in the sky.
Like a jug of water waiting to be poured.
The rain comes down like a torrent of pear drops.
A gust of wind howls like a werewolf.
Storm begins to rage.

*Oliver Manuel (10)*
*Chetwynd Junior School*

## Do You Dream?

One night I went to bed,
I had a dream
About me as a baby,
Trying to walk.
My room was blue tit-blue.
I fell and fell many times,
I started to cry,
I cuddled up to my teddy.
He said
'Hello!
Don't cry.'
He showed me many toys.
I played and played,
But then I woke up
And I said.
'I liked that dream, I wish I could go back.'
But I can remember the bear, he
Had only one eye.

*Rachel Axon (8)*
*Chetwynd Junior School*


## Ocean Dreams

Rain is like an ocean of dreams,
waiting to explode into someone's mind.

At last it falls like a fountain into a
river of silver waves.

But when the sun comes out, the rain
disappears into a gloomy cloud of tears.

*Cassandra Rich (10)*
*Chetwynd Junior School*

## HORSES

A church spire in the distance,
Horses trotting in the meadow
Smelling the flowers,
The golden sun, spiralling, stretching,
Stepping violently down on them.
The blue sky, gleams with the sun shining
Down on the meadow.
Neighing, bucking, rearing,
The pony trotting
Up and down the meadow,
Trying to jump the fence
Which is too high to jump anyway.
The traffic-light yellow stamen so bright
You can't bear to look
Because it disturbs your mind.
The delicate grass,
Looping up out of the ground.
There's a dog chasing a dragonfly.

*Faith Cosgrove (8)*
*Chetwynd Junior School*


## RAIN MATES

Rain diving out of the dingy-looking clouds,
Smacking against the concrete,
Snorkelling in the puddles
Trying to make new mates,
Playing spitball,
Hanging out late at 'Wet Place'
(The local rain club),
Eating Splashages and Wetburgers
With water sauce on.

*Ben Hall (10)*
*Chetwynd Junior School*

## THE SNOWFLAKE SCENE

On a faraway hill,
Snowflakes twist and turn.
On the ground, solid white.
It's cold and wet and gloomy outside.
'Please! Please can I go outside?'
'Make sure you wrap up warm,
and remember to put your gloves on today.'
I go outside and try to catch a snowflake in my hand.
See how long it lasts?
So soft, so gentle.
How long will it last I wonder?
I can see all the detail.
It looks like a spider's web.
It's really cold.
On the ground it's solid white,
Snowflakes twist and turn,
On a hill, far away.

*Danielle Smith (9)*
*Chetwynd Junior School*


## AUTUMN

The autumn starts as green leaves turn brown,
Start to fall, one by one.
The trees are bare, no leaves at all,
The last leaves swiftly fall to the ground.

The atrocious wind starts to howl,
The huge trees, sway,
The gliding leaves glisten,
Seed-pod beige
As they swirl into the night sky.

*Rebecca Lane (9)*
*Chetwynd Junior School*

## MIDNIGHT HORSES

Galloping softly
Through the dusty sand,
Waiting for your turn to arrive.
Here it comes, and you are lapping up
Juicy water from the sea.
Now we are walking through
Sand-dunes.
We might die,
We might live,
Nobody knows.
I wait by the broken gate.
I see a shape,
A biscuit-beige shade,
Moving towards me,
With some sugar, for the
Midnight horses.

*Leah Thiedeman (9)*
*Chetwynd Junior School*


## A LIFE IN THE CLOUDS

Cloud as grey as a winter's day
As dull as the world at war.
Watching, waiting.
Looking over us at every move we make.
Just like gods in the sky, judging us.
Sometimes they cry, they cry the tears of rain.
They flood the sky with sparkling crystals.
Then parachute out into a swamp of sadness.
Deep, deep into a wise, world of sad
depressing fears and thoughts.

*Julie Visgandis (11)*
*Chetwynd Junior School*

## WINTER

There I stand on the garden path,
Looking over my wonderful garden
Full of gleaming, day sky white snow.
The trees are as
White as fresh plain paper.
The sky is a twinkling of
Pale blue light.
As I step forward and stare
Next door I see their tree,
With the looped and swerving branches.
The tree swiftly sways in the breeze,
One way, then the other.
In the distance you can just see the parrot-green leaves,
Gliding and floating away.
But where do they go?

*Christopher Ayers (8)*
*Chetwynd Junior School*


## THE SUN'S EMERGING

The murky, grey storm clouds disappear,
The brilliant, yellow sun is starting to emerge.
Making the deep blue water below, glisten.
The rain ceases,
A rainbow develops,
The glory of the sky.
The thunder and lightning conclude,
The white clouds appear,
Wondrous shapes and sizes
The murky, grey storm clouds disappear,
The brilliant, yellow sun is starting to emerge.

*Matthew Moore (9)*
*Chetwynd Junior School*

## SADNESS

Men in black suits, with no creases, walking, extremely slowly,
Down the aisle with the coffin on their shoulders.
The priest came out of the rear of the church,
Then went to the alter.
The men put the coffin down carefully,
Some went out of the church because they were not family,
The others sat down.
The priest wore his cassock with a gold-leaf cross on the front.
Men and women were crying their hearts out.
When the priest was talking about the person's lovely life.
They all said prayers,
And the funeral came to an end.
It keeps on happening,
Men walking, extremely slowly, down the aisle.

*Chris Johnson (9)*
*Chetwynd Junior School*


## THE CHEETAH

Gentle padding on the crisp grass,
From the beautiful, elegant cheetah.
The roar that breaks your heart.
The crafty creature,
The most
Magnificent
Creature in world.
Here comes the hunter,
A report . . .
The elegant cheetah is
Dead.

*Thomas Leybourne (8)*
*Chetwynd Junior School*

## Meadows By Day, By Night

Meadows by day
will shine their bright light on you.
In the night you will see the moon from
the silver and gold flowers.
In the morning you will be woken up
by the sunshine.
In the night you will hear the wind hitting the
flowers in the field and the meadows.
You will see people running in the red and gold
and silver flowers.
In the meadows, the colours grow all the time,
Day and night and week and month,
All the times of the year.

*Daryl Wilkins (8)*
*Chetwynd Junior School*


## Tornado

It is quiet now.
A welcome silence has fallen.
My house is destroyed,
No house for anyone!

The wind is blowing softly.
The parakeet-green trees are swaying.
Rising leaves rotating, round and round,
Dejected families have departed.
Acutely tense mothers looking for their
scattered children,
Eventually someone says 'Finally it has ended.'

*Jason Holmes (9)*
*Chetwynd Junior School*

## THE SWEET CITRUS LEMON

I watch the sherbet lemon, looking, waiting
It wants to explode and be free from its shell.
When I open it, the sound is loud like a cackle
of a witch
As it twists and turns then unwraps
The yellow sherbet, sweet and sour.
It twisted and turned like a mini explosion
waiting to go off.
As it turned and tangled with my tongue
*Crunch!*
The sherbet exploded, leaving only the shimmering
shock behind.

*Tiffany Rae (10)*
*Chetwynd Junior School*


## WALKING BY THE LAKE

A man and lady
Walking by the lake
With the sun gleaming.
There's an exquisite breeze, so they don't sweat.
The lake is in the country
Where the grass grows high.
Colours, a deep mud-brown and daffodil-yellow can be seen.
The fish from the lake start to jump out and show the meandering
Patterns on their scales.
When the sun goes down, the fish sink back.
The man and lady start to walk home,
To go to their beds.

*Richard Thorpe (9)*
*Chetwynd Junior School*

## SHERBET SENSATION

Staring at the sherbet sweet,
Looking back with glee.
In my mind it is shouting,
'Eat me, eat me, eat me.'

Reaching for the rounded sweet,
Tearing off the wrapper,
A rustling sound in my ear,
As loud as a Christmas cracker.

I put the sweet in my mouth,
It's lemony, yet sour.
This sherbet-filled, tangy sweet,
Is definitely taking power.

I crunch the lemon-flavoured sweet,
All the sherbet fizzes,
The tangy taste sizzles on my tongue,
And down my throat it whizzes.

*Debra Lapworth (11)*
*Chetwynd Junior School*


## RECIPE FOR A RAINBOW

Red for sloppy, wet roses.
Orange, relaxing sunset.
Yellow, swaying, golden corn.
The juiciest green apples.
The blue, colourful sky.
The exotic fish, swimming in the big blue ocean.
Violet for fluttering butterfly wings.

*Tobie Grovenor-Annis (9)*
*Coughton Primary School*

## RECIPE FOR A RAINBOW

Red for a spotted ladybird crawling around your feet.
Orange for a dandelion waving in the breeze.
Yellow for the stars sparkling in the sky.
Green for an apple as juicy as can be.
Blue for a bluebell, blue as the sea.
Indigo for exotic fish swimming in the indigo seas.
Violet for a butterfly in the garden.

*Victoria Lowe (8)*
*Coughton Primary School*


## SMILE

S kinny chicken on my plate.
M usic to dance to in the living room.
I love my parents when they tell us jokes.
L ovely flowers in the breeze.
E very day the sun shines, I smile.

*Rebekah Edwards (8)*
*Coughton Primary School*


## SMILE

S illy brothers that make me laugh.
M any chocolates that I get at Christmas.
I smile when Miss Thomas smiles.
L oyal friends that like me.
E very bit of the world makes me smile.

*Catriona McDonald (8)*
*Coughton Primary School*

## HARVEST FESTIVAL

H erbs are brought to harvest.
A utumn leaves begin to fall.
R oses are spread everywhere.
V itamins make people big and strong.
E ggs are eaten at harvest time.
S ongs are sang at the church.
T urnips are grown in the farmers' fields.

F ish are cut up and eaten.
E veryone loves harvest.
S omeone is looking over us all the time, his name is Jesus.
T ea bags are brought to harvest to make tea.
I t is a glorious place to be.
V ery nice treats are brought along.
A rrivals begin to come.
L ovely lettuce is brought in a salad.

*Rowena Lewis (8)*
*Coughton Primary School*


## SLIMY SEWAGE WORKS

Bold and cold,
coats zipped up tight,
excited to the brim,
murky, slimy, smelly,
a graveyard for sewage,
dirty, smelly, pongy,
slippy slush, sliding away,
scary water, sliding underneath me.

*Richard Perry (8)*
*Coughton Primary School*

## A Recipe For A Rainbow

Red is for the soft
petals on a rose.
Orange is for the
sun sparkling in the sky.
Yellow is for the corn
that is swaying for its life.
Green is for the swaying grass
in a field.
Blue is for the sky
in the morning.
Indigo is for the glistening sea.
Violet is for a butterfly's wing.
Mix it all together and then you have a rainbow.

*Oliver John Arundel (9)*
*Coughton Primary School*


## Rainbow

Red is the colour of a rose swaying gracefully in the garden.
Orange is the colour of a tabby cat, hunting in the night.
Yellow is the colour of a golden sun, shining down on people.
Green is the colour of long, wet grass, moving in the wind.
Blue is the colour of the sky, looking down on us.
Indigo is the colour of a butterfly's wing, fluttering in the air.
Violet is the colour of a lovely flower in my garden, fully grown.

Mix it together and you get a rainbow.

*Jessica Baker (8)*
*Coughton Primary School*

## Animal Circus

Elephants, tigers, hungry bears,
We're all stranded here,
We do tricks and clever things,
just for you humans.
We entertain you day and night.
And we're bored sick!

We could be wild roaming around,
instead we're with you!
We're all lonely, no one to talk to,
But look at you,
Chatting all day while we stay in our cage,
We're bored sick!

*Lauren Jackson (9)*
*Coughton Primary School*


## Recipe For A Rainbow

*Red*     is the blood when you've got a cut.
*Orange* of the twinkling sparklers on November the 5th.
*Yellow*  of the glorious roses beaming in the sunlight of summer.
*Green*   of the swaying grass and the fresh smell when it's just been cut.
*Blue*    of the swooshing sea and children running to paddle in it.
*Indigo*  of the exotic fish, zooming around by coral reefs.
*Violet*  of the lovely colours of the pretty pansies growing in your back garden.

*Thomas Zielinski (9)*
*Coughton Primary School*

## A Recipe For A Rainbow

Red is for pointed, dark maple leaves.
Orange for beaming flames on the fire,
Yellow for skidding slimy butter in a tub,
Green is stiff, hard acorns growing on a tree
sitting in their brown seats,
Blue is nice shining, clean sky,
Indigo of exotic fish shining in the sea.
And last of all,
Violet of a colourful butterfly wing.

All of these colours make a wonderful rainbow.

*Felicity Drinkwater (8)*
*Coughton Primary School*


## I Smile At These Things Like . . .

S ongs that you sing when the sun is shining all the joy they bring for you.
M ost nature makes me smile. When I see animals in nature, I think of all the plants and trees.
I  like it when wild animals communicate however they can.
L ovely flowers make me smile when I look at them. Sometimes they are picked to make bouquets for inside.
E verything makes me smile that's wonderful, beautiful and lovely like my teachers and everyone else.

*Abigail Turk (9)*
*Coughton Primary School*

## DIANA

On a very sad day,
A Sunday it was,
We suffered a death,
A very great loss.

A friend and a helper,
Of rich and of poor,
And now into heaven,
Lord opened the door.

She was loving and helpful,
Loved very much,
By everyone who listened,
Or people of such.

Now up into heaven,
A paradise of truth,
She can do what she loves to do,
Be friends with the youth.

Little children everywhere,
Will miss her a great deal,
While others who knew her,
Will be trying to heal.

She did so much good,
And now we must say,
Goodbye dear Diana,
I promise I'll pray.

Everyone in the world,
Will be torn apart,
With the loss of the princess,
Not just by name
But by heart.

*Karina Lickorish (10)*
*Crescent School*

## THE BLACK HOLE

We're going down a black hole,
I don't know what to do.
My tummy's started shaking,
I feel all sick too.

I can hear strange whirring sounds,
It's going dark alright,
The earth is shaking hard now
In the atmosphere you couldn't
even fly a kite.

I'll say goodbye to the
universe and say
ta-ta to the Milky Way.
It's been great
living on earth.
But now we're going
away!

*Rachel Arch (11)*
*Earlsdon Primary School*

## COSMIC POEM

Last night I saw a shooting star,
It went past me like a racing car,
I made a wish, I wish would come true,
Then I looked up and saw the moon too.
I smiled up at that man in the waxing moon
I knew it would be full soon.
Shining so bright on a constellation,
All I could do, was look up in admiration.

*Sam Green (10)*
*Earlsdon Primary School*

## COSMIC

Why do we bomb our skies,
And kill people as if they are flies,
Why kill our human race, I ask?
The world is like a big, big task,
Why do we spend all our money?
Wasting it on space discovery,
Going up there,
With not a care,
About the people all that matter,
Before the earth turns to a shatter,
We're killing our earth's atmosphere,
Remember it is a sphere,
Not a hollow cylinder like a bin,
Throwing rubbish in a tin,
Soon there'll be no earth at all,
Life is a gigantic fall,
Why waste this earth at all?
Unless we stop there will be none of us at all,
Have you got the message now?
Do something about it now!

*Amy Forse (10)*
*Earlsdon Primary School*


## MY DAY IN SPACE

I went to space in our rocket
To see the stars up above us.

To my *amazement* were the planets,
Mars, Pluto and Saturn.

And suddenly out of the blue
occurred an almighty volcanic eruption.

Which left us no alternative but to do an
emergency crash-landing.

Just after getting our breath back
we found ourselves deserted in the
very heart of Manhattan,

*Rajdeep Sandju (11)*
*Earlsdon Primary School*

## ROUND AND ROUND THE GARDEN

Round and round the garden in my underwear
My mummy doesn't know and the public doesn't care.
Looking out the window, the rain is pouring down,
Got a frown on my face but I'm feeling rather brown.
Wake up in the morning, sun is shining bright
Mum draws the curtains, gives me a fright.
Breakfast is here, sounds like hell,
Head out the window shouting to my pal.
School is a coming, nothing to wear, people keep saying
Have to brush my hair.
People throwing paper, not very nice,
Teacher shouting at them, sounds like Scary Spice.
Making a sandcastle on the beach,
Dad stops the people, Mum makes a speech.
Going to the shops now to buy some stuff,
Mum goes haywire, Dad gets in a huff.
Sister buys an ice-cream, brother buys a kite,
Dad buys some mushrooms but Mum buys a bike.
Poems got to stop now, *hip, hip hooray.*
There's no illustrations but have a nice day.

*Melissa Holloway (10)*
*Earlsdon Primary School*

## Cosmic

Looking down on the great big earth.
With many of its cities like Paris, Chicago
and Perth.

There are birds and bees,
And many, many trees.
There are lots of creatures.
And lots of features.
With its nuclear explosions.
And its polluted oceans.
What is our world coming to?
Is there anything we can do?

Because of pollution, humans are dying
And that is why lots of relations are crying.

Let there be peace on, earth
In all cities like Paris, Chicago and Perth.

*Sarah Davies (10)*
*Earlsdon Primary School*


## Cosmic

They say they're going soon,
You know where I mean . . . the moon.
All they do is pollute the air,
But they don't really care,
As long as they get their share.
They're spending loads on space and rockets.
While people in the Third World have nothing in their pockets.
Who cares if they go to the sun or Mars,
When poor people don't even have any cars.

*Peter Griffin (11)*
*Earlsdon Primary School*

## Universe

I look up to the dark
mist, and all I see is golden
dots and the shimmering of the
silvery moon while shooting stars whizz
through the air. Look up there I see it's Venus
hoping it's not so far between us or maybe
Pluto, Jupiter or some mysterious meteor.
The secrets of the universe
wrapped up in mist begin
to disappear into
*infinity!*

*Georgia Hudson (11)*
*Earlsdon Primary School*


## Space

Every star is miles away,
Billions of miles away.
Astronauts are on the moon.
With a great big boom.
The rocket will take off,
The people will cough,
They will be on their journey,
To the planet Mercury
Soon they will land,
Then suddenly a band
will play a happy tune
from on the moon.

*Alex Bates (10)*
*Earlsdon Primary School*

## Cosmic

If we were plants and trees,
What would we think of us polluting,
And us always looting,
Our planets' riches?

And if all the birds and bees could talk,
They'd all want to walk.
All the dolphins would trade their fins,
Just to stop us killing other things.

If earth spoke, what would it say?
I know *'Stop* all this today!'
'Stop all the polluting and the looting,
or we could give you a right booting
into space.'
'So give up and get a life or earth
Could take *your* life.'

***Phillippa Harvey (10)***
***Earlsdon Primary School***


## The Fall

It is the fall
The golden leaves drift onto the ground
They sit in a smart golden carpet
And they wait patiently to rot.

The dark frosty morning lasts longer
The sunny, long days have gone
It is gloomy with the odd drop of rain
The cool air of the nights draw in earlier.

The fruit is juicy and ripe
The corn is cut in the bright yellow fields
The fresh grassy fields have animals grazing in them
The farmer cuts the old brown, yellowy grass for hay.

So many things happen.
There are too many to say, I can't put them on paper
Soon it will be the end of autumn's turn
The circle of the seasons will move on and
                            winter will come.

*Dominic Bostock (11)*
*Great Alne Primary School*

## CATS

Cats, cats all around,
Making a lovely miaowing sound,
miaow, miaow, miaow
purring quietly making no sound.

Curling up in a corner
quietly by the fire
warm, cosy, soft and fluffy.

That you think he is so quiet
in the house and outside he is wild
and he chases mice and voles.

But really what he likes best
is when he's asleep on my lap.
Well, I stroke him.

When he is asleep he dreams that
he's a wonder cat and becomes a hero.
But when he wakes up he jumps off
my lap and scratches the chair.

*Megan Price (9)*
*Great Alne Primary School*

## WEATHER

It's snowing and the
wind is blowing. Snowflakes
fall to the ground not making
a single sound. Footprints,
Footprints in the ground waiting to be
Found.

It's raining, raining
On the ground. It makes such
A drippy, droppy kind of sound.
In the rain you can run and have fun.
It drips and drops and never stops until the sun comes out.

Look at the sun so hot.
People like the sun a lot.
When the sun is out we like to run and play about.
When the sun shines, people sometimes
Put down their blinds.

The wind is *blowing*
And the leaves are going
    *round*
       *and*
          *round*
              making a kind of howling sound.
The leaves are always found
Lying on the ground.

The frost has come
My fingers go numb
If it's slippy and I
Fall on my bum,
Then I go in and
Tell my mum.

*Kylie Fowles (10)*
*Great Alne Primary School*

## COMPUTERS

I love computers
They're really great
My home computer's
Like my best mate.

It takes me to worlds
That I've never seen
Adventures and islands
Come to life through the screen.

It tests me and
Teases me
At incredible speeds
But all it is, is a bunch of electrical leads.

I've learnt how to program
A bouncy ball game
A quiz for my grandma
Could lead to fortune and fame.

Internet and e-mail
Go through telephone lines
Lots of information
For curious minds.

I've made animations
Out of modelling clay
Monsters and characters
Who run and play.

What I really love
Is computer drawing
So my computer
Never is boring.

*Peter Franklin (10)*
*Great Alne Primary School*

### THE GOLDEN SEASON

Autumn is the golden season,
Leaves fall to the ground.
Forming a colourful carpet,
Gold, orange, red and brown.

Animals will hibernate,
And sleep through till spring.
And wake up to warm sunshine,
Instead of freezing cold winds.

People are out in their gardens,
Raking up the leaves.
And then getting really angry,
As they blow away again in the breeze.

We also celebrate bonfire night,
And we have lots of fun.
Setting fireworks off,
That amaze everyone.

Harvest is here as well,
And we're all in a good mood.
As there's ripe fruits aplenty
And lots of good food.

We celebrate Hallowe'en,
And dress as witches and ghosts.
We also eat lots of sweets,
And that's the part I like the most.

But when autumn leaves,
Winter will come.
But I just love autumn,
Because it's so much fun!

*__Kim Lewis (10)__*
*__Great Alne Primary School__*

## SEASONS

Spring, summer, autumn and winter are the seasons.

Spring is full of new life, like rabbits, flowers and birds.
We celebrate Lent and Easter in spring.
We make pancakes for the beginning of Lent
and give each other gifts of egg-shaped chocolates
for Easter.

Summer comes with happiness, long nights follow.
Sports day comes, your race is next,
it happens in a flash,
the crowd cheers you've won.
The last day comes, no school tomorrow
some people are sad, others are excited,
for a new school awaits us next term.

Autumn brings nothing but rain for this
the animals hibernate, animals like hedgehogs
snakes, mice and fish. Leaves fall down like the rain.
The animals go in and we go out to watch the
fireworks blow. A night to remember when we go out
to trick or treat to scare the living daylights out of
them.

Winter is the greatest season, for we can go out
to play in snow. Sledging down the hill heading for the
barbed wire fence. Christmas is the time of year to celebrate
the birth of Christ. Presents under the tree to feel and
try to work out what it is.

*Chloe Steele (11)*
*Great Alne Primary School*

## HOLIDAYS

Holidays, holidays,
are great fun.
Some are in rain
and some are in sun.

Some are busy,
some are in hills.
For some you relax
or pay big bills.

You lie on the beach
and swim in the sea.
Go to amusements
and waste your money.

Some are cold
and some are hot.
Some are lovely
and some are not.

Some you speak English.
Some you speak French.
Some you speak German.
Some you speak Spanish.
Some you speak Chinese.

Holidays, holidays
are great fun.
Some are in rain
and some are in sun.

***Emily Lavender (9)***
***Great Alne Primary School***

## THE STARRY NIGHT

The stars twinkle
in the sky
like bright little lights.
Sparkling, sparkling
as the night goes on.

The shooting star
flies across the sky
into the darkness.
Sparkling, sparkling
as the night goes on.

The North Star
shines out brightly
helping you to get home safely.
Sparkling, sparkling
as the night goes on.

As I look up I can see
thousands of stars
looking over me.
Sparkling, sparkling
as the night goes on.

Some stars are dull,
some stars are bright,
some stars are big,
some stars are small.
Whatever star it is, I love them all.

*Carly Alder (10)*
*Great Alne Primary School*

## THERE'S A MONSTER IN THE CUPBOARD

There's a monster in the cupboard,
It's green and grisly,
Last night it ate my sister,
And now it's after me.

I run into its cupboard,
It's covered in coloured goo,
Red, orange, green, yellow too.

I hear the monster coming,
Just behind the door,
My only escape is the trapdoor,
In the middle of the floor.

I'll go through the trapdoor,
Maybe it will lead,
To another floor.

I'm going down the tunnel,
There is loads more goo,
It's not orange,
It's blue,
There must be two.

The tunnel is coming to an end,
I've landed bang on the floor,
I see the monsters coming,
There could be twenty more,
But I can only see four.

*Elizabeth Metcalfe (10)*
*Great Alne Primary School*

### A Sleepless Night

In the middle of the night
I looked out of the window
I saw a lighthouse
And stars shining bright

The stars seemed to wink at me
As they caught the light
You could just see the moon
Through the big, old, oak tree

An owl hooted at some cats
Who were chasing all the mice
People who are out late at night
Hide from all the swooping bats

I looked left at the graveyard
I thought I saw a ghost
But instead it was someone crying
He got up and left a card

I looked down at the lawn
Where the grass was full of dew
It sparkled in the moonlight
Although it was nearly dawn

I looked towards the east
Where the sky was turning pink
The birds started singing
Before they had their breakfast feast.

*Jayne Lowe (10)*
***Great Alne Primary School***

## THERE'S A MONSTER CREEPING ROUND DOWNSTAIRS!

There's a monster creeping round downstairs,
Or perhaps a hairy lion that glares,
Going round chewing our kitchen chairs,
With a face so ugly it scares!
        Scares!
        Scares!
There's a monster creeping round downstairs,
On this dark, dark night,
So I'm holding my duvet so tight!
        Tight!
        Tight!
Do I dare to go down and turn on the light,
Or am I best to keep out of sight!
        Sight!
        Sight!
There's a monster creeping round downstairs,
Perhaps it's green and as broad as a beam,
And it's not to be seen
Because it's so mean!
        Mean!
        Mean!
There's a monster creeping round downstairs,
Perhaps it's got fangs and it's making those bangs,
That thump and that bump!
        Bump!
        Bump!
There's a monster creeping round downstairs!

*Mariska Wilkins (10)*
*Great Alne Primary School*

## FOOD!

Tea will be ready in a
flash,
What are we having?
Sausage and mash!

Pears, eclairs and of course
jelly,
Bananas, sultanas they all fill my
belly!

Tomorrow I think we will have
meat,
It's not a surprise but it will be a
treat!

A bit of a pip flew out at me,
It came from an orange that was very
juicy!

On Wednesday for tea I had
stir-fry,
and then for pudding I had
apple pie!"

For lunch tomorrow I'll have a
pancake,
Unfortunately they make my
tummy ache!

***Victoria Gow (9)***
***Great Alne Primary School***

## 1998 IS GREAT

It's 1998
This year's going to be great.

I'll fly across the ocean,
go diving under the sea,
see fish and crabs,
and a big white shark
this year's going to be great.

I'll plant some flowers,
big sunflowers,
daffodils, roses,
in the sun
this year's going to be great.

I'll eat fruit and nuts,
great big bars of chocolate,
lollies, ice-creams,
melting in the sun
this year's going to be great.

I'll have a Christmas party,
with balloons and streamers,
games and carols,
sweets and mince pies.
1998
was great.

***Charlotte Onslow (9)***
***Great Alne Primary School***

## ZOO ANIMALS

Look at the zoo animals,
They are lying on the floor,
Thinking of how they used to live,
And to be wild and free,
But instead have to be watched.

Patiently they wait to be free again,
To play with their brothers and sisters,
But instead have to play in the mud and dirt,
Their food is served on plates,
But in the wild they would kill their own food.

The monkeys swing on ropes and tyres,
But in the wild they would swing in trees,
Eating fresh fruit from the branches,
They are watched by parents and children,
But would you like to live in a cage with
everyone watching you?

Animals don't deserve this,
They want to play with their brothers and
sisters again,
And kill their own food,
They don't want to live in a cage,
Why can't you see,
That the animals want to be free?

*Gareth Price (10)*
*Great Alne Primary School*

## SCHOOL DINNERS

We're waiting in the dinner hall
in a long, long queue,
'You're not allowed to push now
Kate, that means you too!'

'What are we having for lunch today?'
'I don't really know!'
'No one else knows Miss
and the menu does not say!'

'Did you say roast chicken and roast potatoes Miss
that's my favourite meal!
If you give it me every day Miss
you will have yourself a deal!'

'If we have dinners like this all the time Miss
I will be on cooked dinners every day,
If anyone asks me to go back on packed lunch
my answer will be *no way!*'

I wonder what dinners would be like in the old days?
Probably carrots and lumpy custard
with a little bit of horseradish sauce
and maybe spicy mustard!

I would prefer dinners now they're nice
because we have things like curry and rice.

*Laura Clark (9)*
*Great Alne Primary School*

## THE ALIEN TEACHERS

When the children have all gone home,
There is a low and solitary drone,
A spaceship lands on the school field,
Then the teachers come out all holding shields,
To stop passers-by from seeing their faces,
As they make their way towards the spaceship.

The rocket goes,
It blasts right up,
Then the alien teachers,
Boy, they sup,
On slaughtered kids' brains
Then the limbs,
They throw the rest away down the drains.

Then when they land,
On their planet X3,
They shout out *'Hooray, yippee,'*
We've got away from those ghastly kids,
Who eat nothing but slimy squids.

Then they pull out their super laser blasters,
And back at the school,
They jump upon the rafters,
Waiting for the children to return.

*Thomas Smith (10)*
*Great Alne Primary School*

## DOGS

Dogs can be hairy and very scary,
Some have fleas,
Some chase bees,
Some hate cats, some sleep on mats,
Some are tall,
Some are small,
Some like to play with bouncy balls.

Dogs love to run and have lots of fun,
Some dogs are lazy and some dogs are crazy.
Some are happy, some are sad but there are a
few who are very bad.

Dogs can be fat and some love to have a pat
after they have been good.
Dogs make a mess they couldn't care less
where they put their muddy feet.

Dogs can be young, dogs can be old,
Some dogs are as good as gold.
Dogs love to eat a lot of juicy, tender meat.
Some dogs howl, some dogs growl,
Some dogs lie curled up in a ball,
But I have a dog who's the
    *Best of all.*

***Emma Lealan (11)***
***Great Alne Primary School***

## 1998 THE NEW YEAR

1998 it's great
it's a happy time to
celebrate.

Parties, fun and
games to play,
On the night before
*New Year's Day.*

Dancing
Singing,
Inside and out,
Listening
to the
people
*Shout.*

I think the
*New Years*
are great
especially staying
up very late
and seeing
in
1998!

***Becky Stanton (10)***
***Great Alne Primary School***

## My Pet Guinea-Pig

My pet guinea-pig
eats lots of carrots.
She wheeps and squeaks
like a parrot.

My pet guinea-pig
likes to have a run.
She loves and loves
the big, hot sun

My pet guinea-pig
has a brother.
They always wheep
at one another.

My pet guinea-pig
is really sweet.
She always eats greens
and never meat.

My pet guinea-pig
is quite big.
But she isn't really
a big, fat pig!

*Katie Lamburn (10)*
*Great Alne Primary School*

## FLASHY LIGHTNING

Lightning thinks it's flashy
as it streaks across the sky
it's bright and ragged
light and jagged
very, very high.

It comes and goes with thunder
as it rolls along the sky
bright and ragged
light and jagged
very, very high.

Thunder does not like it
so it grumbles all day long
bright and ragged
light and jagged
very, very high.

Thunder thinks it should be banned
lightning thinks that it should stay
bright and ragged
light and jagged
very, very high.

*Jennifer Hawkins (10)*
*Great Alne Primary School*

## The Infant School Play

'Thomas dear, don't make faces.'
'Elizabeth, Dawn, stand in your places.'
'Katie don't pick your nose and for
goodness' sake don't wipe it down your clothes.'
'Chloe love, go to the loo.'
'Richard, you're a sheep so please don't moo!'
'Amelia dear, please stop shouting.'
'Natasha, you're an angel so please stop pouting.'
'Megan, don't hit the boys, you're not to hurt
them, they're not toys.'
'Kimberley, have you wet your pants?'
'Ashleigh, stop doing that silly dance.'
'Emma Jayne, please stop crying.'
'Miss, Peter hit me,' 'No I didn't, he's lying.'
'Dominic, Gareth, don't hit the girls.'
'Victoria, stop pulling Emily's curls!'

*Jodie Evans (10)*
*Great Alne Primary School*


## I Wonder...

What is it like up there in the sky at night,
Is it dark, is it grey, is it light, is it bright,
When I lay in bed at night,
I wonder.

What is it like up there in the sky at night,
Where the stars lay all night,
Do they play or do they stay,
When I lay in bed at night, I wonder.

*I wonder... I wonder... I wonder... zzzzzz.*

*Elizabeth Kelly (10)*
*Harbury Primary School*

## JOURNEY THROUGH SPACE

I went to space in a rocket
to see the stars and the moon.
Soon we were in orbit
I felt light as a balloon.

There was a big mistake
we ended up on Mars.
There was another problem
we'd forgotten the space cars.

We climbed out of our rocket
but to our dismay.
There was another rocket
It was blocking our way.

Two men brought us into their rocket
it went up in the air.
We were heading back to earth
Then we all just started to stare.

The rocket was flying towards
a very big rock.
I ran to the control panel
there was little time left on the clock.

I panicked and pressed a button
not knowing what it would do.
Luckily it was the right one
away from the rock we flew.

We landed on earth safely
with a lot of pleasure.
People were asking questions
this trip I'll certainly treasure.

*James Armitage (9)*
*Harbury Primary School*

## UP THE BLUES

I'm a Coventry supporter
I love to watch them play
And if I didn't go to school
I'd watch them every day

I'm a Coventry supporter
I love to sing the song
About the great Blue Army
I feel that I belong

I'm a Coventry supporter
My favourite's D Dublin
When the ball is chipped up high
He jumps and heads it in

I'm a Coventry supporter
I'd love to see the day
They win the cup at Wembley town
And I will shout hooray!

*Thomas Wilkins (9)*
*Harbury Primary School*


## COSMIC

I watch the stars at night
Twinkling in the sky
Reflecting in the sea so bright
In the day they're a little shy
Millions shining like crystal
Hunter, his dog, Gemini
And many more, so beautiful
In the day, invisible in the sky.

*Ben Kluth (10)*
*Harbury Primary School*

## MY FRIENDS

I've got a friend called Stacey
Sophie's my friend too.
I've got lots of friends just like them
Here are just a few.

Elli and Maria
Sitting learning in the class.
Elizabeth and Ashley
Playing football on the grass.

Katy and Nadia
Like dancing in the park.
Carley and Antonia
Are frightened of the dark.

We all go to Harbury School
This poem could bring me fame.
All my friends like helping me
And Alison is my name.

*Alison Shepherd (10)*
*Harbury Primary School*


## WHEN I FALL OUT WITH MY FRIENDS

It's when I come home that I can feel sad,
Something inside me that's making me mad,
I know what it's like to be really hurt,
You're like some kind of species of dirt,
That's why I won't hurt other people,
It makes you feel like you are lethal,
All I want is a big, big cuddle,
Make up with my friends and get out of this muddle.

*Elli Bristow (9)*
*Harbury Primary School*

## ALIEN DAYS

I twinkle like stars and shine like the sun,
I glitter like tinsel. Boy, space sure is fun.
As I fly 'round the world in the blink of an eye,
Zooming through space way over the sky,
I watch pink lemonade stars go by.
I'm an alien, don't you know, in my snazzy flying saucer

I visited earth just yesterday,
Crash-landing in a bale of hay
My teacher says I should work on my descent
He says that's why my spaceship gets so bent!
I'm visiting lots of places, and when the day is done
It's 'goodnight' to Hale Bopp
(knocking everything over as he goes
How he got his licence, no one knows)
And I'm off home.

*Ashleigh Henry (10)*
*Harbury Primary School*


## WORKING WITH DAD

I like to go to work with my dad
it makes me happy, never sad.
He wakes me up at half-past six
to help him go and lay some bricks.

When the wall is halfway done
we have a tea-break, a drink and a bun.
Then back to work to make the wall higher
and home to sit in front of the fire.

*Ben Baldwin (9)*
*Harbury Primary School*

## Cosmic Journey

Three, two, one, lift-off.
Silver metal glinting in the sun.
The rocket exploding into the sky,
Zooming through the clouds to the solar system.

Blazing a path from the earth,
To reach red, dusty Mars,
A shooting comet shimmers near the moon,
Far away, Saturn with gigantic rings,
Tangerine orange.

The burners are turned off,
The rocket slows down,
Coming to a stop on Mars' volcanic craters.
The little green aliens have come home.

*Peter Smart (9)*
*Harbury Primary School*


## Perry The Panda

Perry the Panda is short, small and stumpy,
Walking along a log, very, very lumpy.
Her very favourite food is bamboo sticks
Which all day long she licks and licks and licks.
She has a very favourite friend called Ken
Who has a very best friend called Ben.
They all live together in a small yellow house.
Which another friend built, called Mouse.
She has a long, pink tail and she lives in a pail.
She eats red and yellow jam
And lots of egg and Spam.

*Nadia Bowyer (10)*
*Harbury Primary School*

## COSMIC

Black, black is space
Just look at the moon's face
Shooting stars whizzing by
Look at that rocket flying high

The sun so bright, it hurts my eyes
Aliens flying around like flies
Jupiter's twirling
Saturn's whirling
Mars tastes like a chocolate bar
Looking good so far.

The Milky Way, white as ever
Not going to space again -
Never!

*Alex Corkhill (9)*
*Harbury Primary School*


## MY GRANDMA'S DREAM

My grandma's dream was strange,
She dreamt she flew up to space,
She rode on stars,
To get to Mars,
She jumped on Jupiter,
(She thought she got stupider,)
She landed on Pluto,
Didn't want to stay there,
So then she awoke,
And thought how lucky she was,
Living on earth . . . Earth!

*Katy Grimshaw (10)*
*Harbury Primary School*

## COSMIC CITY

Busy cars jammed up together.
Tired dads going home from work.
Litter in the street bouncing and somersaulting.
Boy gangs blocking shop doors, smoking cigarettes.
Millions of red, shining lights which can be seen at
the other end of the street.
Stray dogs, acting like wolves, howling and hunting
in dustbins.
Poor, ragged, homeless teenagers living in cardboard boxes.
Police sirens echoing to every corner of the city.
Police cars chasing burglars at supersonic speed.
Car engines revving and car wheels spinning.
Tyres screeching with a smell of burning.
              *Crash!*

*James Smart (9)*
*Harbury Primary School*


## I WENT TO MARS

I went to Mars to see the stars
The moon and the Milky Way
The sun was bright in the night
As I travelled through the day

Mars is like a chocolate bar
Saturn spinning in its rings
Silver stars, yellow ones too
Twinkling, sparkling looking for you.

I went to Mars to see the stars
The Universe is cosmic.

*Megan Nannfeldt (10)*
*Harbury Primary School*

## My Mom Always Burns The Toast

My mom always burns the toast
She does it on Sundays the most
She ends up standing on a chair
Wafting a newspaper in the air
The smoke alarm is really loud
Set off by the big, black cloud
Dad comes down holding his nose
in such a graceful pose
He opens the door and lets fresh
air in
I just stand there listening to
the din
At the end of it all, what a sin
The toast goes in the bin.

*Lee Bettelley (10)*
*Harbury Primary School*

## My Poem

I saw a spider yesterday,
He said to me 'Come out to play!'
He was quite round and he was hairy,
In fact, I thought he was quite scary.
His legs were long, but one was gone.

I thought this sad, until I saw,
Him run with ease, across the floor.
Then up the wall I saw his web,
And inside that, I saw his bed.
Trapped in this web I saw a fly,
And that's what made him say goodbye!

*Maria Houghton (9)*
*Harbury Primary School*

## Cosmic

Lots and lots of stars
are twinkling in the sky.
Oh, I wish I could fly.

In the galaxy I would be
Exciting planets I would see
As big rockets zoom past me
Then I'd feel really free.

Then I wake up in my bed
feeling really sad.
Because it was all a dream
in my head.

*Jack Hawkes (9)*
*Harbury Primary School*


## My Shadow

My shadow's sometimes tall,
My shadow's sometimes small.
My shadow's like a ghost,
When the sun begins to roast.

My shadow's very thin,
Although it's got a big, big chin.
My shadow's like a ghost,
When the sun begins to roast.

When my shadow vanishes away,
I hope it comes back another day.
My shadow's like a ghost
When the sun begins to roast.

*Liz Murray-White (11)*
*Ilmington CE Primary School*

## PEACE

Poppies swaying from side to side,
Happiness everywhere,
White crosses remembering everyone,
Happiness everywhere.

Messengers coming to bring peace,
Happiness everywhere,
Families rejoicing to be together,
Happiness everywhere.

People starting to love one another,
Happiness everywhere,
Hope coming to life,
Happiness everywhere.

Shaking hands with your enemies,
Happiness everywhere,
Friends together again,
Happiness everywhere.

Fathers seeing their children again,
Happiness everywhere,
Mouths saying 'War is over,'
Happiness everywhere.

*Charlotte Wright (11)*
*Ilmington CE Primary School*


## GOODNIGHT

Sitting on my window-sill,
Listening as the night grows still.
As the pale, full moon comes round,
From behind the dark grey cloud.

Night, so quiet and still,
What's the point in day at all?
See the shadow of the church tower, tall,
Peaceful, quiet, lovely and still.

*Caitlin Hanrahan (10)*
*Ilmington CE Primary School*


## THE LANCASTERS OR THE DAM-BUSTERS

The Dam-busters fly at night
When, over in Germany, it will be light.
Machine guns loaded,
Bombs ready,
This ride won't be very steady.
As they approach the dam,
They hear a big *bam!*
Messerschmitts come out
And try to take them out.
Machine guns roar,
The spent cartridges litter the floor.
'Eight down, three to go.' shouts the commander,
'Hurry up, don't go slow.'
A bomb goes off,
Misses the dam - but not a lot
Two planes go down,
Only to be shot.
One Lancaster flies down,
Lets its bomb go:
It goes like a ball,
Rolling through snow.
*Boom!* The dam breaks,
The Lancasters fly home,
Remembering their mates.

*David Griffiths (11)*
*Ilmington CE Primary School*

## TREES

The fluffy, mischievous fir,
Going so fast you see just a blur,
Always where he isn't wanted,
Never wants to go to bed,
He always plays roughly with his toys,
He is the worst of all the boys.

The tall, beautiful birch,
To find one more beautiful you would have to search,
Miles and miles around the world,
Because of her bark so white and pearled,
And yet she has a heart of stone,
No wonder she is so alone.

The whitebeam is new in town,
Her voice is such a beautiful sound,
She's even more beautiful than the birch,
She's so dainty, she would never lurch,
Only tip-toe round about,
She's kind and her hatred's nowt.

The ash is lovely whitebeam's husband,
He came from a distant land,
So he is new as well as her,
He loved the girl - the way she twirled!
He was kind and gentle too,
Oh, the things that he could do.

The strong, kind oak,
By the water his branches soak,
The king of trees - yes he is,
That strong trunk could only be his,
Very old and wise is he,
His strength anyone can see.

*Lois Stamps (9)*
*Ilmington CE Primary School*

## FELIX - (WONDER CAT)

My cat called Felix
Has been in the Olympics.
He's been king in Arabia,
And flown to the moon.
His coat is always purr-fect
He says so himself.
He's in every subject
We do at school.
The teachers all love him
That's a real pain
They're *always* praising him.
It's always the same.
'Why don't you be a good child
like lovely old Felix is?'

I never get praised.
I'm jealous because of that.
When I get home from school
He's there on Mum's lap,
Reading poetry to her.
I slump into a chair
And tell Mum about school
I'm never helpful.
Mum always complains.
Whatever she says to me
It's always the same.
'Why don't you be a good child
like lovely old Felix is?'

*Daisy Blacklock (10)*
*Ilmington CE Primary School*

## OUR FLY

Our fly in the kitchen,
Flying round and round.
*Buzzing, buzzing, buzzing.*
What an irritating sound.

Our fly in the living room
Settles on Dad's head.
Poor little fly,
I bet he'll soon be dead.

Our fly in the bedroom
Narrowly missed the swat.
Sleek body, shiny wings,
He's got the lot.

Our fly doing somersaults,
What a clever fly.
Landed in a spider's web,
Then he'll soon be in a pie.

He was our fly . . . !

*John Griffiths (11)*
*Ilmington CE Primary School*


## COVENTRY CITY

The players coming fast and bright,
Passing the ball with all their might,
Huckerby runs into the wing,
He passes the ball to my best player Dublin.
He heads the ball with all his soul,
Everyone cheers, it was a goal!

*Becky Foster (11)*
*Ilmington CE Primary School*

## WATER

Trickling down the stream it flows,
Through the hedge,
Glistening in the warm summer sun.
I come out to play,
On a warm summer's day,
And watch the stream flow by.

Down comes the rain,
Smashing on the road,
Banging on the car,
Washing in the gutter,
I rush inside to get dry,
And sit by the fire.

*Timothy Smart (9)*
*Ilmington CE Primary School*


## CHILDREN OF WAR

I see the children of war, dying and thin,
I see the children of war, and cry within.
The children are poor, they aren't well-dressed,
Please help these children, it's up to us.
I see the children of war, hopelessly weak.
I see the children of war, and hide - dare I peek?
The children are sick, they're nearly through.
Please help these children, it's up to you.

*Kate Holberton (11)*
*Ilmington CE Primary School*

## WATER

I hear water dripping,
I see children skipping,
I pour water in my drink,
I don't like pink,
I see water running down the lane,
It rains.

Water running down the rooftop,
I want the water to stop,
Water splashing,
Water flashing,
Water is very precious to us,
I see water dripping from the bus.

*Hannah Kerby (11)*
*Ilmington CE Primary School*


## NIGHT-TIME

I'm afraid of night-time:
It's spooky, dingy and dark.
There's lots of creepy-crawlies
Who come out to play and lark.
I stay awake and tremble,
Afraid they'll tear me apart
And give a wicked laugh.
Night-times are
Spooky, dingy and dark.

*Peter Griffiths (11)*
*Ilmington CE Primary School*

## THE FALCON

The hungry falcon sits on his branch.
Suddenly his ears twitch.
What is it?
He flaps his wings and takes off.
He glides through the air.
Like a hot knife through butter.
He glides down.
As fast as a bullet.
He swoops up carrying a vole between his claws.
The falcon feasts on the vole.
Now he's not hungry.

*Jim Sipthorp (11)*
*Ilmington CE Primary School*


## MY CATS

My cats are called Milly and Molly
They are both very jolly.
Molly is tabby and white and is very bright
Milly is a blue tortoiseshell.
When she is wet she feels like gel.

Milly is so silly
Molly is so jolly
When it's night they like to fight
When it's day they like to play.

*Rebecca Brewster (10)*
*Ilmington CE Primary School*

## TRACTORS

Tractors
*Brumm . . . brumm . . .*
Tractors run
Through the meadows
Far away
Feeding the cows
Feeding the sheep
Now the lambing season has begun
More work for the farmer
*Brumm . . . brumm . . .*

**Will Brundle (10)**
***Ilmington CE Primary School***

## THINGS FROM SPACE

Things from space,
We don't know what's in space,
There might be aliens,
There might be animals,

There could be people up there,
There could be food and water,
Like grilled piranhas with bananas!
We don't know but I'd like to know.
About things in space.

**Athena Pantazievits (10)**
***Ilmington CE Primary School***

## My Dog

My dog is quite big and tall,
and has a big rubber bouncy ball.
He plays with it in the garden,
and he gets it stuck up a tree.
When it's soggy and wet
he gives it to me.

*Liam Edden (10)*
*Ilmington CE Primary School*

## Number 4

At number 4 in our street,
You'll never guess what happens.
By the light of a street lamp nearby,
Number 4 shows at its best.

We hardly ever go near in daylight,
But we never go near at night.
'An old man lives there.' says Mum.
'But does he?' says everyone.

I'll tell you a story about last night,
I awoke with a sudden want of fresh air.
I went to my window and I got a terrible fright,
What I saw and heard was like a nightmare.

The window opposite me lit up by a candle,
A figure silently crept past.
A noise almost stopped my heart.
I ran to my bed. Very fast!

'You never know it might have been rats.' says Mum
'But was it . . . ?' says everyone.

*Emily Hensman (11)*
*Keresley Newland Primary School*

## NIGHT

The night is dark and
the moon is shining
and bats are creeping
and the cats are moving.

The weather is moving
in the sky the twigs are breaking
and creaking and
foxes are hunting.

The trees look like people
and the dragons are
roaring and breathing fire.

It looks really scary.
It sounds like the rain
is touching the water
and the spider makes webs
and the bats are in the moon
and the people are singing
and the wolves are howling
and the white eyes are scary
and the chickens are making an noise.

*Andrew Wood (10)*
*Keresley Newland Primary School*


## INNER SPACE

As we fly into inner space
The large planets' red, gleams on my face
I see the shooting stars' orange glow
They fly above me and below
We start to go very far
*Whoosh* there's another shooting star.

The silence of the galaxy
You'll be surprised what you can see,
Gaseous mists, asteroids, the black hole,
So inner space is really, a lump of coal.

Inner space, inner space
The excitement shows on my face.

*Carla MacDonald (11)*
*Keresley Newland Primary School*

## NIGHT

Silently sleeps the world
As night is here
The silver, shining moon
peeps into the windows of people's houses.
He lights up all the world.

The shimmering grass was a
sparkling silver.
The shadows of the big enormous trees
looked really frightening.
I could hear the bushes shaking.

Shadows on the walls of people's houses
All you could hear was the footsteps
of people walking by.

As the moon goes down and the sun rises
everything in the world lights up.

*Laura Mandara (11)*
*Keresley Newland Primary School*

## NIGHT AND THE DESERTED HOUSE

Night comes on
Sun goes down.
The night-spirited creatures
They're howling, screeching, creeping,
Restlessly up to the house.

Moon's like a torch
In the dark you see
The figures stealing
Things in the moonlight.

The house vanishes in the
light of the moon.
Changing all the time to
gold and silver.
Night goes by.
The sun draws on.

*Faye Randle (10)*
*Keresley Newland Primary School*


## NIGHT

Night roams the land
like a gang looking for
trouble,
his battle awaits
him,
but does he know?

He covers the land
like a bed-cover
spreading all over.

He prowls forward
then he strikes,
but dawn is more
powerful,
her light kills him.

Darkness is no more.

*Karis Dalziel (10)*
*Keresley Newland Primary School*

## I SEE...

I look around, I see swirling, shining,
gleaming, sparkling, shooting, whirling,
golden, sparkling stars.
I look around, I see gigantic, enormous,
bulging planets, bulging into the horizon.
I'm standing upon a blue planet, there's
bright orange, lime-green and yellow, red,
purple, silver and gold, flowing into the
empty space.
I feel afraid, scared and frightened.
As I look around in fear, I feel a
shiver shoot up my spine.
I feel lonely and deserted.
I hear nothing, silence, quiet and noiseless.
Suddenly I hear the sound of shooting stars
zooming by.

*Louise Thomas (11)*
*Keresley Newland Primary School*

## MUSES

Darkness receding back into
the corner.
The silvery river turning
to colour.
The river coming to life
floating away with a current.

The sun rising level with
the dark brown trunk.
The sun an orange, yellow,
golden colour.

Animals running to and fro.
Squirrels peeping in and out
the tree holes.
Fish swimming fast and quickly
coming to a white bubbly waterfall.

Night-time enveloping over us.
All the animals running to their
homes.
Every colour in sight turns to black.
The sun goes, goes down,
The river turns to silver and slows down.

*Danielle Eddy (11)*
*Keresley Newland Primary School*

# NIGHT

Things are coming out tonight,
Scurrying mice,
Darkness enveloping the ground,
we walk on,
Robbers racing house to house, car to car,
Bats resting their wings,
Owls flying tree to tree as they hunt,
Grass as silver as the moon,
on the ground,
that we walk on,
And all the ghosts flying house to house
house to house.

*Gary Whittle (10)*
*Keresley Newland Primary School*


# WHY CAN'T GIRLS PLAY!

I read in the newspaper
*Footballer wanted*
It was my dream to be a footballer
It said meet at Coventry stadium.

I raced down to the stadium
But when I got there
There were no girls
And there was the manager

'Excuse me what are you doing here?'
'I'm here for the job'
'Sorry football's a man's job, go to the ladies' team.'
Why can't girls play (in the men's leagues)?

*Laura Maton (9)*
*Mount Nod Primary School*

## FAST CARS

When I grow up I'll drive fast cars
zooming round the country lanes
and bolting down the motorways.

I'll drive Ferraris, Porsches too
even BMWs but most of all
I'd like to drive a bright red Lamborghini.

*Ben Tyler (11)*
*Mount Nod Primary School*


## IN THE SAD WAR

I hate wars they are really bad
When people get shot and killed it is really sad,
When children go the countryside to stay
I know I would miss friends and family every day.
Some people are big, some people are small,
Some people don't miss their family at all.

*Dean Thomas Wilson (10)*
*Mount Nod Primary School*


## SCHOOL'S BORING

School is very boring I think you'll all agree.
Design and technology is not the subject for me.
Art is very boring I think you will agree.
PT is OK, though it's not my cup of tea
Assemblies are boring, they make me fall asleep.

*Sam Moore (10)*
*Mount Nod Primary School*

## SNOOKER MATCH

How much is it? I ask.
Twenty pence the sign says.
That's how much it is to play,
Upon the green baize.

First a red
And then a pink.
What's the next ball,
He has to sink?

Another red!
This time a green.
Balls going down
No more to be seen.

What next I wonder.
Nothing left to pot.
Another game maybe,
Perhaps I'll get a shot.

*Peter Green (10)*
*Mount Nod Primary School*


## THE SIMPSONS

The Simpsons are neat.
The Simpsons are cool.
The Simpsons are driving me up the wall.
The Simpsons are having just as much fun
if I was eating a juicy bun.
Macavaty doesn't like me nor does Homer.

But I don't like the Flanders!

*Stephen Horton (10)*
*Mount Nod Primary School*

# GHOSTS!

They creep around behind me,
I'm as scared as scared as can be,
They cry behind me and wriggle up,
I drink from out of my really big cup,
I look behind, there's no one there,
Except the moving breeze of the air.

It *roars* and *roars, aaargh,* I scream,
It's the ghosts of the old football team,
      *Aaaarrggh,*
It's them, it's them, it's them, it's them
It's them, them really big, fat men.

They're really, really fat,
They look like a big, big bat,
They're big and bold
and all they did all day
they *scared.*

**Sammie Fisher (9)**
**Mount Nod Primary School**

## PUPPIES

Puppies are fun
Puppies are bad
They chew up the furniture
They're just so mad
They bark all day,
They bark all night.
Can't we just send them
On a one-way flight!

**Athena Ashmore (10)**
**Mount Nod Primary School**

## CATS

There are big cats,
Little cats.
Fat cats,
Thin cats.
Black cats,
White cats.
Brown cats,
Grey cats.

There are funny cats,
Boring cats.
Cute cats,
Horrible cats.
Noisy cats,
Quiet cats.
Tame cats,
Wild cats.

*Carly-Ann Bury (11)*
*Mount Nod Primary School*


## ALIEN

Three antennae topped with lights
Spiky shoulders in greens and whites
A huge rubbery mouth without any teeth
A big pot belly with a kilt underneath
A long, grey beard that reaches his toes
One glowing eye on the end of his nose
A handsome beastie I'm sure you'll agree
He is where he comes from, the planet McZee.

*Joe Chamberlain (10)*
*Mount Nod Primary School*

## THAT'S ALL THEY WANT

Down the dark alleyway,
Under a tall truck,
In the pouring rain,
The cats want a shelter,
That's all they want.

They look so shabby,
And miserable,
All they want is a home,
With lots of love and attention,
That's all they want.

By a fire, purring softly,
Tummies full of food,
Dry and warm,
Safe and sound
That's all they want.

*Laura Bass (10)*
*Mount Nod Primary School*


## BOOKWORM

Babe's delicious, really meaty,
Enid Blyton's a real sweetie,
Roald Dahl, rather tough,
Books on running, leave me out of puff!
Books on veg are hard to find.
Because I leave them far behind!
Books on mines are a real blast,
So get to your local library . . . *fast!*

*Hugh Clayden (10)*
*Mount Nod Primary School*

## SET THEM FREE!

The tiger wearily prowls softly,
around his tiny enclosure,
with a sad, grim look on his face.
'It isn't right!' I say, I say,
'It isn't right' I cry!

These creatures they belong in the wild
Not! Not! Ever! In a cage, a tiny, tiny cage.
So set them free I pray, I pray,
Set them free to be.

Then the tiger won't wearily prowl
softly around his tiny enclosure, he will,
Run! Run! Run! Go! Go! Go!
Out into the wild with his
friends and *foe!*

**Kirsty Brooks (9)**
**Mount Nod Primary School**


## ALL BECAUSE PEOPLE WANT MONEY

Elephants are killed for all the wrong reasons,
Killed for their tusks so people can make money,
Elephants should be left alone,
To have a happy life.

Just think of the babies now orphans,
All because people want money,
We should protect, not kill,

All this happens because people want *money*.

**Sammy Cossey (10)**
**Mount Nod Primary School**

## THE STROKE OF MIDNIGHT

*It* was dark on the stroke of midnight,
Quiet on the stroke of midnight,
And cold on the stroke of midnight,
A robber came over the hill.

*It* was dark on the stroke of midnight,
Eerie on the stroke of midnight,
And loud on the stroke of midnight,
A gunshot rang out loud and clear.

*It* was dark on the stroke of midnight,
Frightful on the stroke of midnight,
And at the foot of the hill,
The robber lay in his blood.
And at the foot of the hill,
Stood the Redcoat troop, tall, proud and still.

*Bart Daly (10)*
*Mount Nod Primary School*


## DOLPHINS

Dolphins swimming freely in amongst the waves,
Gliding swiftly over deep, blue waters,
But they get caught,
Nowhere to swim,
Nowhere to hide from hunters,
Cooped up in tiny spaces,
Banging their flippers on the surface of the water,
Making clicking sounds or whistles.
    *Dolphins become*
        *extinct.*

*Lois Jones (11)*
*Mount Nod Primary School*

## WORK

I like technology,
I've never tried biology,
Maths is boring,
Everybody's snoring.

We make a car powered by an elastic band,
Teachers say 'Hard footballs are banned.'
PE is cool,
On Tuesday in the swimming pool.

Breaststroke, diving all the rest,
The boy next to me is the pest.
Keyboards play 'Rock Around The Clock'
Off on Friday with chickenpox.

*James Tuck (9)*
*Mount Nod Primary School*


## WHALES

There are no whales in Wales
Isn't that a pity.
For I would go and visit them
The whales in Wales.
Whales are beautiful beasts of the sea
Navy like the waves.
They spout water from their backs
The whales that I wish were in Wales
But there are no whales in Wales
In Wales there are no whales.

*Amy Clarke (10)*
*Mount Nod Primary School*

## HUNTING!

It was icy but the fox needed its food.
The fox ran through the icy, frosty woods,
but who, I say who? Is waiting at the
other end?
That man with bristly beard,
with a gun in his hand.
The fox scampered through the rain
but it is too late . . .
*Bang!*
Down goes the fox.
Killed by that bristly man with
the big gun.

*Nicole Lane (10)*
*Mount Nod Primary School*


## THE FOX-HUNTER

He rides out on the horse to shoot a fox,
But does he care, I think not.
He sends the dogs after them
To catch them for him to kill.
He sends the dogs after them
So he can shoot them dead.
It's easy for him, he thinks,
But he doesn't care about foxes out there.
He despises people who protest against the cruelty;
He thinks they are senseless,
Because he doesn't care about foxes out there.

*Emma Stowe (11*
*Mount Nod Primary School*

## BONFIRE NIGHT

flames burning
orange and red
catherine wheels
spinning shimmering
lights flames waving
hissing wheels
colours flashing
stars popping
screamers screeching
popping and banging
from the sky.

*Katie Tamplin (8)*
*Nursery Hill Primary School*

## BONFIRE NIGHT

wood crackling
shooting sparks
shimmering flames
popping colours
happy laughing
ashes snapping
cold wind
black smoke floating in the air.

*Leanne Tucker (7)*
*Nursery Hill Primary School*

## WAKE UP!

Mum shouting,
Slamming door,
Ticking alarm clock,
Birds singing,
Buzzing door bell,
Telephone ringing,
Vrooming cars,
Dogs barking,
Hissing cats,
Taps dripping,
Splashing milk.

*Leah Moore (8)*
*Nursery Hill Primary School*


## FIREWORKS

Big sparks shooting up to the sky
children laughing in excitement
lots of shapes
colours up high in the sky.
Crackling and screeching,
shooting all around.
Holding a sparkler writing your name,
rockets whooshing up to the sky.

*Tom Betteridge (8)*
*Nursery Hill Primary School*

## WAKE UP

Birds chirping,
Mum talking,
Door slamming,
Loud music,
Water dripping,
Postman's steps,
Mum shouting,
Clock tick-tock,
Milk splashing,
Dogs barking.

*Gemma Bradbury (8)*
*Nursery Hill Primary School*


## FRIENDS

Friends can be awful
Friends can be nice
Friends can be sweet
As sweet as sugar and spice!

Some friends are really bad
Some friends can make you sad
Some friends across the street
Have really bad smelly feet!

*Danielle Radford (9)*
*Nursery Hill Primary School*

## WAKE UP!

Mum talking,
Ding dong bell,
Slamming doors,
Kettle whistling,
Teaspoon whirling,
Toast crackling,
Paper crinkling,
Money tapping,
Banging footsteps,
Milk bottles clanging.

*Hannah Jones (9)*
**Nursery Hill Primary School**

## ANCIENT EGYPT

In Egypt there are some lovely places
Where you can find gods with strange faces.
I like a Pharaoh called Tutankahmen,
Who had jewels and furniture in his tomb.

Mummification is the thing I hate,
As people are thinking about their fate.
I love the pyramids because they're tall,
But be careful if you climb one because you might fall!

*Greg Shearing (10)*
**Nursery Hill Primary School**

## WAKE UP

Bird tweeting,
Kettle whistling,
Microwave popping,
Loud snoring,
Rain pitter patter,
Wind *shh shh*,
Cars *vrooming*,
Crunching Rice Krispies
Dripping water,
Letter-box slamming.

*Naomi Beasley (8)*
*Nursery Hill Primary School*


## BONFIRE

Fire flames in the sky
wood crackling on the fire
Ashes burn in the fire
flames dancing in the sky
Hot fire burns the wood
smell the smoke around
The crowd of people
the fire dies and the crowd
goes home.

*Jack Northall (7)*
*Nursery Hill Primary School*

## WAKE UP!

Shouting mum,
Whistling postman,
Creaking staircase,
Sisters snoring,
Parents yawning,
Toilet flushing,
Neighbours squabbling,
Slamming doors,
Smashing teaspoon,
Rick Krispies crackling.

**James Isaacs (9)**
**Nursery Hill Primary School**


## SPRINGTIME

Springtime will soon be here
Birds fly by and the air is clear
The flowers start to grow
And the farmers start to sow
In their fields this time of year.

I like the springtime because it is a fun time
The skies are blue, the nights become light
This gives me a chance to play out on my bike
These are the best things about springtime I like.

In springtime my dad takes me fishing
One thing about winter that I am missing
My mum's birthday is in springtime
That is why springtime is the best time.

**Shelley Hardcastle (7)**
**Race Leys Junior School**

## Snow

White, soft and crunchy
from up above
swirling and twirling
cold, icy and windy.
Don't forget your
warm cosy hat,
and of course don't forget your gloves.
You don't want to have your scarf on, it tickles all your neck,
but Mum's nagging again so I had to wear my scarf
that tickles my neck.
We pulled our wellies on and rushed outside to have some fun
rolling snowballs and throwing them at your mum!

*Fern Brown (10)*
*Race Leys Junior School*


## Aliens

Aliens are green with 3 big googley eyes,
Or purple with eyes big and bright.
They fly through space in UFOs,
Looking at Earth below,
Watching us humans
Dance, run and play football all day long!

*Rachel Walker (10)*
*Race Leys Junior School*

## UFOs

They whoosh and wizz in the air,
They flash their lights everywhere,
They take everybody by surprise,
If you see one you won't believe your eyes,
They spin and turn round and round,
They make an amazing buzzing sound,
They're purple, red, green and blue,
But are they old or are they new?
So while they're dazzling in the air,
You'll never know what might come out of there.

*Cara Palmer (10)*
*Race Leys Junior School*


## Spring

The wind blows strong across the hill
And slaps the yellow daffodil
And the red wavy trees and the
Sharp crinkly leaves remind the farmer
To plant his seeds in the brown earth
Where the old roots stir and early
This morning the small birds sang.

*Jade Hill (9)*
*Race Leys Junior School*

## Dolphins

In the clear blue waters of the sea,
swims a beautiful animal called a dolphin.
Twisting and turning through the waves,
doing no harm in any way.
Their smooth grey body jumps in and out of the water,
showing off for people to see.
Why do people want to hurt them,
when they don't hurt anybody.
So please don't hurt them,
leave them to play in their playground.

*Rickey Carter (8)*
*Race Leys Junior School*


## The Kite Fights

The kite fights with the wind
it fights and it fights till the end.
It always loses or does it?
The kite loses.
The kite loses against the wind.
I do not believe it do you?
Oh no the string has come off my kite,
now I believe it.

*Josh Neale (8)*
*Race Leys Junior School*

## Winter

Winter is near, now winter is here.
We dress up warm, wellies as well.
Snow on the ground, snow all around
Snowball fights all over the place.
Watch out or you'll get hit in the face
It might sting a bit, but do not worry,
Do not cry just hurry, hurry.
Soon you're warm with a cup of cocoa
but before you know it you're dying with laughter.

*Amy Ann Hill (10)*
*Race Leys Junior School*


## Dolphins

Smooth, gentle and caring.
Diving, gliding all alone in the clear blue ocean.
Every day they watch the sun rise then settle.
No one to play or dive with. A sad gloomy world
for us but a dream and adventure for them every day.
When the wind goes by they can hear the sound of
dolphins calling them to play but the sound goes
on forever and ever, until it fades into another
ocean and that's another story.

*Lauren Wayte (9)*
*Race Leys Junior School*

## MY PET PIG

My pet pig
Sits on a rock
He's not very big
Just about the size of my sock.

My pet pig
Has only one leg
He lies on his back
Doesn't sit up and beg.

My pet pig
Lies sunning himself
Through wind and rain
Just like an elf left on a shelf.

My pet pig
Mum digs and sows
While my pet pig
He just lies while she mows.

He's not real he's not
Of course
You see
He's made of pot.

*Abigayle Hendry (8)*
*Race Leys Junior School*


## FROST

It slowly falls to the ground,
It sparkles then it clutches to a tree,
It sprinkles in the air round and round,
Then it disappears out of sight from me.

*Aimee Cotton (10)*
*Race Leys Junior School*

## Seasons

Birds are chirping
Lambs are bleating
Flowers are opening
Leaves are bursting
Blossom is flowering
*Spring is coming.*

Sun is shining
People swimming
Sandcastle building
Children paddling
Picnic gathering
*Summer is coming.*

Leaves are falling
Wind is blowing
Rain-clouds forming
Fireworks sparkling
Faces glowing
*Autumn is coming.*

Jack Frost biting
Snow is falling
Fires burning
Carol singing
Turkey roasting
*Winter is coming.*

***Jenny Marshall (7)***
***Race Leys Junior School***

## THE BIRD

With his tail pointing straight
And his wings stretched wide
He flies through the air
With ease and pride.

He looks all around
For worms and things
He dives to the ground
'I've found my dinner' he says.

He sings in the morning
He sings at night
He's a wonderful creature
The bird in full flight.

*Ian Gough (7)*
*St Anne's RC Primary School, Nuneaton*


## THE ZOO

One day at the zoo
Orang-utans were big, hairy, and ugly too!
Lions big and fierce with a scary face
Prairie dogs underground digging all around
Meerkats standing high looking in the sky
Sea lions dive to catch a fish
So much to see and do at the zoo!

*Ashley Mears (8)*
*St Anne's RC Primary School, Nuneaton*

## FA Football Cup

It was the big day
We went to the Villa
The game was exciting
In fact it was a thriller

We scored a goal
I shouted out loud
When we had won
I felt so proud.

*Craig Sweeney (8)*
*St Anne's RC Primary School, Nuneaton*


## The Space Town

There was a town on the moon
Where swimming pools were craters
In shopping malls they sold
Remote-controlled moon-buggies and anti-gravity suits
There was a space and sea rescue shuttle
And everybody wanted to boldly go
Where no man had gone before.

*Jamie Wyatt (9)*
*St Anne's RC Primary School, Nuneaton*

## NIGHT ANIMALS

Some say that night is quiet.
When the sun is away,
the moon comes out.
While all is at rest,
but not all.
Foxes prowl and wild dogs howl,
cats stalk, barn owls swoop
silently making not a sound,
their wings like silk,
drifting on a cloud.
Mice run about on their
dainty little feet,
aware of the hunters,
they hope they will not meet.
Morning is coming,
the sun is in the sky.
The night animals hurry home,
before the moon says 'Goodbye.'

*Gemma Pamment (10)*
*St Faith's CE Junior School, Alcester*


## SOMETIMES

Sometimes I feel happy,
Sometimes I feel sad,
But changing my brother's nappy,
Really makes me mad,
I wish I didn't have to,
It really is a pain,
But let me remember,
I love him all the same!

*Becky Chester (11)*
*St Faith's CE Junior School, Alcester*

## My Busy Street

As I plod down the cobbled street,
I feel the smooth and bouncy tarmac,
Beneath my feet.
I see the nattering,
Chattering folk,
I see the distant steam train,
And its smoke.
The baker calls,
The florist bawls,
The fishmonger clatters about.
Cars shoot by,
No one gives a sigh,
The day hurries on!
Workmen whistling,
Sausages sizzling,
The smell carries,
Over to me.

*Jennifer Howes  (11)*
*St Faith's CE Junior School, Alcester*


## Springtime

S  pring is a happy time,
P  eople always feeling fine.
R  aining now, no fear,
I   f it does I'll hide in here.
N  ow is the time to go and play,
G  o on, play all day.
T  rees blooming in the sun,
I   f you fall, hug your mum.
M  ummy calls you in for the night,
E  nd of the day so tuck up tight.

*Hannah Muitt  (9)*
*St Faith's CE Junior School, Alcester*

## APRIL SHOWERS

I sit in front of the television,
With nothing else to do.
The rain is pouring down outside
Like it has done for two days running.
The news says 'It's the worst in years
And that it does not want to stop,'
But I just hope we can have some sun
After all it is April.

Hooray it's finally stopped!
And the sky is looking blue,
The sun is out and shining bright
As merry as can be.
I'm glad we have some sun at last.

*Jessica Harrison (10)*
*St Faith's CE Junior School, Alcester*

## CATS

Strolling through the bushes,
Prowling round at night.
Walking over rooftops,
Completely out of sight!

Playing in the hay bales,
Chasing mice galore.
Hearing food bowls rattle,
Darting through the door!

Sleeping by the fire,
Cosy in a ball.
Or curled up in a basket,
Peaceful in the hall!

*Naomi Blayney (10)*
*St Faith's CE Junior School, Alcester*

## Santa Claus Is Coming

Santa Claus is coming
he is bringing sacks of toys,
he used to bring some for me
and put them under my Christmas tree,
but now I have no daddy
and he never comes to me.

I sat there in silence
wishing for Santa to come,
when I hear the flutter of angels' wings
I heard the noise of church bells ring,
I sat there in my tattered rags
and who had come
it was my great grandad.

He wasn't a mortal
he was an angel from heaven above
he told me of the Christmas dove,
the dove is white,
the dove is gentle,
the dove is a little white bird of love.

*Christine Wilkinson (10)*
*St Faith's CE Junior School, Alcester*


## The Homeless Man

The poor old man has no money
Standing in the street.
He has no family and has no friends
And he also has nothing to eat.

So next you see the poor old man
Standing in the street.
Think of the poem I've read to you
And give him something to eat.

*Anne Gould-Fellows (9)*
*St Faith's CE Junior School, Alcester*


## THE WEATHER FORECAST

The weather forecast
says 'It's cold this morning,'
The weather forecast says
'It's dull.'
The weather forecast says
'It's going to snow this week,'
but I don't believe anyone!

The weather is sunny this morning,
so the weather forecast must be wrong.
The weather forecast is a liar,
so never believe in it!

The weather is sunny this morning,
so the little lambs are born,
they are so sweet this morning,
that my heart is torn!

The weather forecast must
have got it all very wrong:
it is so hot this morning
that I could put a cossy on
to dance in the street with bare feet!

*Olivia Beeson (10)*
*St Faith's CE Junior School, Alcester*

## THE TIGER

The tiger walks elegantly,
With his heart full of pride.
Slowly, slowly,
With soft gentle strides.

His heart lets off,
A quiet beat,
As he stalks,
Something to eat.

His paws touch the ground,
Slowly, so slowly,
And make, not a sound,
Softly, so softly.

As he draws near,
Silently, oh so silently,
He hasn't a fear,
As he draws near.

His heart starts to pound,
Quickly, quickly.
It's getting quite loud,
And much quicker, quicker.

He's getting ready to jump,
Slowly, so slowly.
His heart's started to thump,
Strongly, so strongly.

Eventually he's caught it,
Hip-hip-hooray!
And now he's eaten every bit,
And left only the bones!

*Hip-hip-hooray for the tiger!*

**Penelope Sarah Eileen Mills (10)**
**St Faith's CE Junior School, Alcester**

## ME

My hair is red
My eyes are blue
My nose is big
My mouth is too

My dad is mad
My mum is sane
My cat is fat
My friend is Jane

My car is red
My bike is blue
I like to ride
My friend does too

I like my school
I like my friends
I know I'll be sad
When this year ends

My teacher is sweet
His name is Pete
My friends say
He has smelly feet.

**Claire Wood (11)**
**St Faith's CE Junior School, Alcester**

## Cosmic

5, 4, 3, 2, 1, *Blast off*
Stars go shooting by,
Aliens in their flying saucers
Wave and say *'Hi!'*
In the magical world above Earth,
*It's Cosmic!*

As we race in our rocket past Mars,
We see aliens shaped like jars!
Then suddenly I spot Venus
The aliens there,
Quite a few were square
And some had fur like a bear.

The aliens on Uranus
What a fright they gave us,
They were purple and green
Some as thin as a bean
Never have I seen
Such aliens as I saw on Uranus.

Next we flew on to Jupiter
Where the aliens were so much stupider
Than any I had seen
I don't think they could have been

More stupid if they had tried.
My story is not a lie.

*Sarah Grant (10)*
*St Faith's CE Junior School, Alcester*

## Mornings
*(Dedicated to my big sister, Jessica)*

In the dark, dark morning,
When everyone is yawning,
I hear a moaning and a groaning.
Everyone is shaking,
With fear.

'What could it be?'
'Don't ask me!'
The noise comes once more.
It could only be a monster,
So ugly.

A hunched-back, blotched and dotted,
A face rough and spotted,
Eyes bulging out like golf balls,
Arms all scaly,
And green.

I had always felt,
That I would melt,
This monster felt so close,
In only the,
Next room.

I lately found,
That this ugly mound,
Was not what I had thought,
This horrendous monster,
*Was my big sister!*

**Sophie A Merrick (11)**
***St Faith's CE Junior School, Alcester***

## THE SEASON

In the spring,
the lambs play,
the daffodils come out.
The sun is hot
and sometimes it rains.
The spring is nearly over and the
*Summer* has come.

In the summer,
the paddling pool is out.
The bluebells sprout up
and the sun is hot
sometimes it rains
The summer is nearly over and the
*Autumn* has come.

In the autumn
the people are out
the leaves fall down
and the wind is cold
it rains a lot
The autumn is nearly over and the
*Winter* has come.

In the winter
the children are out to play
the trees look bare
and the wind is cold.
The snow falls heavily.
The winter is nearly over and
*Spring* is back again.

*Louise Foy (9)*
*St Faith's CE Junior School, Alcester*

## EXECUTION
*(July 12th, 11.23)*

He came there on a summer's day,
The sun soon caught his eye,
A sun can live forever more,
But men are sure to die.

The sheriff did not look at him,
He tried not to, he turned his eyes,
But the man who would live no more,
Glanced once more at the sky.

A bird that flies above the clouds,
Can be looked at once again,
But the gold rays of the sun,
Are riches still to men.

He has not wished to walk this way,
He had no wish to die
Men will live by rules and laws -
But their hearts may fly.

The gold he'd taken from the church
Had turned to grey dust when
The guards had come and taken him away -
He relived the scene again.

He mounted on the prisoners' cart
Looked at the sky once more.
The clouds were open, sun shone down -
The way to heaven's door.

He did not speak unto the priest
But the hangman's deed was done:
The sheriff looked up to the sky
A bird flew into the sun.

*Harriet Bradley (9)*
*St Faith's CE Junior School, Alcester*

## SPRING IS GREAT

Spring is great, bright colours everywhere,
I love spring, it's the best season,
Spring is great, animals out of hibernation,
Sweet little squirrels hunting for shiny, brown nuts,
Bright yellow, red and blue flowers,
In pretty shapes and patterns, all around us,
Lovely, pink blossom, on towering, brown trees,
People with cheerful, happy faces, plants grow tall,
Spring is a time when sun never disappears,

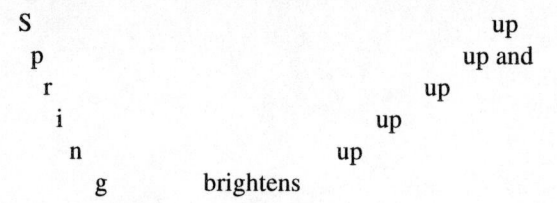

```
S                              up
 p                              up and
  r                          up
   i                      up
    n                  up
     g      brightens
```

*Ian Maguire (9)*
*St Matthew's Bloxam CE Primary School, Rugby*


## DAFFODILS

Daffodils, daffodils, sunshine yellow
Daffodils, daffodils, pretty handsome yellow
Daffodils, daffodils, wide awake
Daffodils, daffodils, so attractive
Daffodils, daffodils, drifting by
Daffodils, daffodils, beginning to die
Daffodils, daffodils, sinking slow.

*Reena Tank (8)*
*St Matthew's Bloxam CE Primary School, Rugby*

## SUMMER DAYS

Children playing in the orange sand.
Teenagers sunbathing on bright yellow beaches.
Children having fun in the great paddling pool.
Splash, splash, splash.
Bright orange red sun in the blue sky.
Children spraying water at each other.
Spray, spray, spray.
Children running around the colourful garden.
Run, run, run,
Children playing football on green fields.
Children climbing wavy trees.
Wave, wave, wave.
Children throwing balls to each other.
Bounce, bounce, bounce.

*Emillie Jones-Cutter (8)*
*St Matthew's Bloxam CE Primary School, Rugby*


## THE CREATURE

A creature came from space.
I saw it float and land,
I saw it with my eyes
Coming from his spaceship
It was green, silver, red and blue.
He made me go flimsy and scared.
I made him afraid and speechless
I saw an alien, out of space
I saw it with my eyes.

*Rita Chauhan (8)*
*St Matthew's Bloxam CE Primary School, Rugby*

## SUMMER

Flowers sway softly
Through green grass,
They twirl quickly
As I walk past,
Golden sunshine lighting
Up the world,
Butterfly, butterfly flying past,
Spreading its wings and flying past,
Raindrops falling
Drip, drip, drip,
Sunshine blazing on flowers,
On flowers,
Butterfly flutters in the sky,
Fluttering, fluttering in the sky.

*Aysha Khurshid (8)*
*St Matthew's Bloxam CE Primary School, Rugby*

## PE

Curling, twirling, rolling about,
Stretching toes and feet,
Moving, jumping all around,
Different movements all the time.
Pulling muscles when you stretch,
Hopping, rolling on the floor,
Spinning round, round and round,
Enjoying PE all the time,
Doing PE with a friend.

*Jayna Mistry (9)*
*St Matthew's Bloxam CE Primary School, Rugby*

## SWIMMING

Beautiful butterflies flying around
Golden honey bees flying down.
Children diving, splashing
Water swiftly moving
Children on slides
Going head first, tumbly, tumbly
*Down,*
    *Down,*
        *Down.*
Bubbles appearing, water getting deeper!
Boards on the water
Children fighting to get one
There they go, flying underwater
    *Splash.*

*Nathan Woolery (9)*
*St Matthew's Bloxam CE Primary School, Rugby*


## SNOW

Snow, snow
Go away
Come back
Another day,
*No!*
*No!*
Don't want to,
I will let you spray snow,
(Your snow is falling)
Frost glittering,
Icicles cracking.

*Scarlett F L G Chamberlain (8)*
*St Matthew's Bloxam CE Primary School, Rugby*

## RAIN

Raindrops splash
Raindrops splash,
Down they fall,
Down they crash,
Silver drops sparkle, splash,
Falling, falling not stopping,
Silver water, splash,
Drip, drop, drip, drop
                drop
                     drop
                        splash.
It's splish, splashy,
Splish, splosh, splash.
                        I love rain.

*Katie Morse (9)*
*St Matthew's Bloxam CE Primary School, Rugby*


## FLOWERS

Flowers sparkling in sunshine
Glazed by moonlight
Giant sunflowers in gardens.
Flowers all different colours.
Pretty flowers.
I love flowers.
I like flowers,
Lovely petals on flowers.
What lovely golden flowers.
Yellow flowers in the soil
Flowers, flowers, flowers.
Oh how I like flowers.

*Hayley McGowan (8)*
*St Matthew's Bloxam CE Primary School, Rugby*

## FISHING

Fishing, fishing, fishing,
Fishing's the best sport
Casting the rod out
On the calm pond
Catching wet silver fish
Like carp and roach
The sun goes down
We pack up and
Settle down
To bed   z
         z
     z
 z

*Andrew Miles (8)*
*St Matthew's Bloxam CE Primary School, Rugby*


## THE SEA

The sea blew swiftly and silently,
Across the sand so soft,
Children building sandcastles,
Then pulling the flags off.

The sea blew roughly and loudly,
Across the sand so hard,
Children running away crying,
It's knocking the sandcastles
        d
            o
                w
                    n

*Katie Beattie (8)*
*St Matthew's Bloxam CE Primary School, Rugby*

## SKY BLUE CRAZY!

Huge crowds cheering,
As players jog on,
Everyone shouting
Sky-blue hats on.
Darren Huckerby on the ball,
Learnt his skills
Brilliantly at school,
It's Darren on the ball,
He dribbles all the way,
He lobs the ball over
Peter Schmeichel,
And into the net.
'1-0, 1-0, 1-0,
1-0, 1-0, 1-0' shouts the City crowd.
'Boo!' shout the Man U fans.
'Andy look, quick,'
Now it's Cole on the ball.
City crowds with faces down,
But they know City,
            Will never go down.
Crowds waiting for the
Second half whistle to go,
Man U won't win,
No, no, no.
'2-1 to the champions,
2-1 to the champions,'
Shout the City fans.

*David Simpson  (9)*
*St Matthew's Bloxam CE Primary School, Rugby*

## WEATHER

One day it's cold
Then it's warm,
One day it's autumny,
The next day it's bold.
It could be wintry,
One day it's mild,
The next few days,
It's gone all wild!
Summer, summer,
All month bathing,
In the golden sun,
Playing all day,
Fun, fun, fun,
Winter, winter
Sleigh, snowballs,
White snowmen,
Up to the clouds,
Winter is over,
Snowmen melting down.
Autumn, autumn
Grey, brown leaves
All they do,
Is fall off trees.
Spring, spring,
Flowers, popping up,
Daffodils, roses,
And buttercups,
Springing everywhere.

*Daniel Gelston (8)*
*St Matthew's Bloxam CE Primary School, Rugby*

## RAINDROPS

Rain go splish,
Rain go splosh,
Down they fall,
Down they drop.

Rain comes soon
Not at noon
drip,
 drip,
  drip,
Then go splish.

Like a tap,
In the sky
drip,
 drip,
  drip
Then go by

Splishy, splashy, splishy, splash,
I love floods,
When they crash.

*Priya Mistry (8)*
*St Matthew's Bloxam CE Primary School, Rugby*


## SPRINGTIME

Snowdrops cover the ground with a white carpet,
Daffodils start to peep through the grass,
Lambs are leaping on the grass of the meadow,
Birds are starting building their nests.
Crocuses are starting to grow on the lawn,
Everybody, spring is *here!*

*Melissa Forman (8)*
*St Peter's CE Primary School, Nuneaton*

## FRED!

When I was quite young,
I had a fish called Fred.
He was very small,
his scales were bright red.

He lived in a big tank,
With plants that were bright.
He had a pot castle,
to sleep in at night.

And then one day,
When it was sunny.
I had a strange feeling,
inside of my tummy.

I ran to my house,
I opened the door.
I looked at Fred's tank,
and then at the floor.

I knelt on the floor,
I looked at poor Fred.
His eyes were wide open,
I knew he was dead.

So the very next day,
We buried poor Fred.
His eyes were still open,
his scales were still red.

I took one last look,
At his scales shining red.
I started to cry,
and I miss my poor Fred.

***Elizabeth Morton (10)***
***St Peter's CE Primary School, Nuneaton***

## DEVOTED FRIEND

All day I sit still and wait,
For someone to come up the drive.
To close our big garden gate,
For someone to arrive.

All day I wait for others,
I long to hear their voice so much.
Sitting on the thick covers,
I long to feel their touch.

All day I wait and think,
About the days that have gone by.
How that ducks float and don't sink,
And how that birds can fly.

Then at eight o'clock at night,
I listen extra, extra hard.
I really think that I might,
Hear something in the yard.

I can hear a voice down there,
I think as I lay down my head.
I look up into the air,
Then wriggle into bed.

Then the door opens slightly,
And the shape of my friend I see.
He comes and hugs me tightly,
Then he goes down to tea.

His dark shape again I see,
As he takes off his jumper red,
And tightly more he hugs me,
Then he curls up in bed

*Jenny Mepham (11)*
*St Peter's CE Primary School, Nuneaton*

## SPACE

Rockets blast off into space,
By the moon they flew.
Just about to lose their race,
But *hooray* they drew.

We passed Mars that is so red,
Then we stopped to see.
We also found some red lead,
And it was shaped like me.

Astronauts doing their thing,
Bouncing up and down.
Neil Armstrong is the moon king,
And you've got a frown.

Shooting stars in the sky,
As bright as can be.
In the sky so very high,
Just as you can see.

The big bang created stars,
And of course the earth.
But remember the planet Mars,
The big bang gave us birth.

We are in the Milky Way,
The sun gives us heat.
And we need the light for day,
And it hurts your feet.

**Sophie Sutton (11)**
***St Peter's CE Primary School, Nuneaton***

## PETS

Fat dogs, thin dogs,
Dogs that eat like wart-hogs.
Dogs that eat like little pups,
Muck around and jump up.

Dogs that play fight,
Dogs that snap and bite.
Dogs that run away,
Dogs that sleep all day.

Dogs that have fun,
Roll about or lie in the sun.
Dogs that do their best,
At the end need a rest.

Tall cats, small cats,
Cats that try to catch rats.
Cats that eat a lot,
Cats that jump on the spot.

Cats that scratch you,
Cats that like something new.
Cats that stay in bed,
Cats with a little head.

Cats that have fun,
Lie about in the sun.
Don't move in the heat,
Cat that's fast asleep.

*Emily Brooke (11)*
*St Peter's CE Primary School, Nuneaton*

## 13 TODAY

6am ducks in the pen
rabbits in the hutch
then mayhem.
Mummy shouts
'Who let Moriarty out?'
Camilla whines
'He's got wet paws,
get that cat back indoors!'
Rabbits loose in the hoose.
Chewing gum, sucking her thumb.
Off to school Camilla won't wait
Jonquil's going to be very late.
Jumps in the garden
let's have some fun
dog food out the bin
let's annoy Mum.
Tracy and Sharon all awash (the fish)
the water's all cloudy golly gosh.
Toothpaste 'round the basin,
flannel not rung out
clothes scattered on the floor
school books spilling out.
Mummy shouts more and more
there's nail varnish on the floor.
End of day Home and Away
tantrum time, quarter to nine.

*Felicity Sargent (9)*
*St Peter's CE Primary School, Nuneaton*

## GROWING UP

When I was 0 years old,
I didn't do a lot.
I slept all day and slept all night,
In my cosy cot.

When I was 1 year old,
I had a big surprise.
I was in a competition,
And I won first prize.

When I was 2 years old,
I began to walk and walk.
Then I learnt some words,
And began to talk and talk.

When I was 3 years old,
I went to playschool.
All I did was play,
I think that was the rule.

When I was 4 years old,
I went to a proper school.
Then we went on a trip,
Mickey was a fool.

When I was 5 years old,
I was in year 1.
Then I met a playful friend.
And his name was John.

When I was 6 years old,
I was in year 2.
Now I get some homework
And lots more to do.

Now I'm 7 years old,
I am in year 3.
Now you know about a person.
And that person is *me!*

**Natalie Horton (9)**
***St Peter's CE Primary School, Nuneaton***




## SEASONS

S ummer is full of happiness sitting on sands so warm.
   Licking those runny ice-creams whilst sitting on the wall.
E aster we like because of chocolate and Easter eggs so sweet.
   We get fatter by the pound and chubby-cheeked.
A utumn is when the leaves turn red, gold and crispy. They fall down
   like a leaf storm. I like to run through with my feet going
   crunch, crunch, crunch.
S pring is when lambs are born, I see them run and jump. Lots of
   lovely daffodils pop up. It is a peaceful season with scenery so
   bright. Lovely flowers all around, it really is quite bright.
O ne more day to go then Christmas will be upon us. We've got the
   Christmas tree up with presents all around. I just can't wait,
   I've asked for a Nintendo. My sister's asked for a flute,
   I suggested something more exciting like Scalextric for instance.
N ovember keeps the fun of bonfire night with sticky toffee apples
   and fireworks so bright. I like the rocket stars, the green ones
   especially. Berni our dog, has to go indoors, he gets frightened
   otherwise.
S o that is all the seasons. I know which one I like best, it's got to be
   winter, what's yours?

**Laura Teece (9)**
***St Peter's CE Primary School, Nuneaton***

## MY DRAGON

My dragon's got flaming eyes
they look like jewels sparkling
in the sun.
When it's dark his eyes glow
like coloured stars dancing in the
dark atmosphere but his body's still
unseen, hidden in the black blanket
of atmosphere.
My dragon's got millions of gold scales
covering his magnificent body but his
magnificent tail and his beautiful wings
are dyed in a flaming purple.
He isn't slimy, he's very dry and rough.
My dragon's swift and noiseless
he flies like a feather and if you
ever see him all you will hear is
his soft breathing and the soft
flapping of his gentle wings.
My dragon's the best of them
all.

*Rowenna Chartres (8)*
*St Peter's CE Primary School, Nuneaton*


## IF I HAD A MONSTER

If I had a monster
this is what I'd do
I'd cut you up in pieces
then he'd eat you.

*Felicity Melia (7)*
*St Peter's CE Primary School, Nuneaton*

## RUGBY POEM

As I am down in the scrum I wish for my mum,
I see all the players dressed in layers and I say my prayers,
Mauling and rucking I hope I don't get a booking,
The balls thrown out and without a doubt the crowd will shout out.

As I run down the pitch it's like falling in a ditch,
I am covered in mud, cold, thick and brown which makes me frown,
Now I am back in the scrum I think I must be dumb,
I think there must be a game which involves a lot less pain.

I shout at the ref . . . but I think he must be deaf,
While standing on the wing I hear the hooker's knee go ping,
As he screamed out loud I turned and looked at the crowd,
As the stretcher came on we wait for the game to go on.

As we clap our mate off we prepare to kick off,
Then as we started to play the ball was thrown my way,
As I started to run I thought this could be fun,
As I dive for the try line I realise it's the wrong line.

*Wayne Saunders (10)*
*St Peter's CE Primary School, Nuneaton*


## FOX

Rusty-red with a snow-tipped tail,
and a nose as black as night.
Darting eyes looking into the skies.
Waiting.
Waiting for a rabbit or hen to come by.
Then suddenly he moved and walked away
into the darkness of the night.

*Verity Hatfield (8)*
*St Peter's CE Primary School, Nuneaton*

## FROM MARS TO DEATH

Shooting stars,
Planet Mars.
The Black Hole,
Is in my soul.

It's the moon,
Be there soon.
The bright stars,
The fading, red Mars.

A black world,
With no light,
Suddenly,
Everywhere's bright!

The sun, sun,
It's so bright,
Too much light!
I'm burning, burning . . .
*Dead!*

*Nick Vennart (10)*
*St Peter's CE Primary School, Nuneaton*

## SPRING

Spring is when baby animals are born.
Lambs are leaping over the spring meadows.
Daffodils poking out of the fresh green grass.
Spring is a time when we have fun.
We all like spring, so why not come and play
with us in the lovely springtime.
*Spring is wonderful!*

**Kyan Cheng (9)**
***St Peter's CE Primary School, Nuneaton***

## The Pencil Tin

The pencil tin is hungry,
Waiting to be fed;
At last it spots a victim,
'A pen,' the tin said.

The tin now has a short rest,
Sitting on a book;
I check that it's in the bag,
It gets roughly shook.

Soon it's finished the journey,
It is feeling grey;
Then it gently falls asleep,
Until the next day.

*Tom Kelly (10)*
*St Peter's CE Primary School, Nuneaton*


## Fireworks

Fireworks flying
Fireworks diving
Fireworks spinning
Fireworks spitting
Fireworks go round and round, up and down
Sparkling, sparklers, sparkle in the night, rockets fly up *Bang!*
They blow up, bangers bang, children laugh, bonfires burn
Celebrate for bonfire day.

*Luke Bonser (10)*
*St Peter's CE Primary School, Nuneaton*

## Cosmic Travels

Flying through the universe,
Past the cosmic stars,
Stopping to get out your purse,
You're gonna go to Mars.

Meeting all the cosmic things,
Stopping for a chat,
Flying with their super wings,
Moving like a cat.

Bored of all the Marsy stuff,
Time to move along,
Helmet on, the ride is rough,
After that I'm gone.

*Meg Donaldson (10)*
*St Peter's CE Primary School, Nuneaton*


## The Pond

At the bottom of Fish Lane,
There is a pond of 6
I find it quite insane,
That the fish eat Weetabix!

They're small and scaly fish,
Four Golden Orf and two,
They're not my favourite dish,
And they don't like you!

*Rebecca Boston (10)*
*St Peter's CE Primary School, Nuneaton*

## THE KILLER WHALE

It splashes through the water
Like a giant shooting star.
It whistles in the wind,
So gentle and soft.
Its skin is so black,
As black as coal.
Its tummy is so white,
Shining like the moon.
I'd love to see a killer whale
Splashing in the sea.

*Rachel Cardani (8)*
*St Peter's CE Primary School, Nuneaton*


## SPRINGTIME

S pringing lambs, jumping to and fro.
P retty blossom on cherry trees.
R ushing rabbits in the long grass.
I ce is melting before people's feet.
N aughty chicks making havoc.
G olden trumpet of the daffodil.
T oads are jumping with joy.
I mmaculate new green leaves.
M any animals come out this time.
E vening air smells like a lovely spring.

*Matthew Goodwin (9)*
*St Peter's CE Primary School, Nuneaton*

## The Temple Mayan

I have seen the temple Mayan,
in the early morning,
all is very peaceful and still,
the kookaburras are chattering,
the sun peeps out from behind the cactus plants,
it shines down on the temple,
but then . . .

A bang and a clatter!
Out come all the people, they go up the steps
of the temple, there are hundreds on it.
Later in the morning you will hear
with all the buzzing and chattering,
*Screams*!

It is of the people being sacrificed
by the priests.
I know this because I sometimes watch.
They pull their hearts out,
I just think they are strange,
but I am just a monkey,
watching the sun come out from behind the cactus plants.

*Melanie James (9)*
*Stivichall Primary School*


## My Best Friend

He has a smile on his face like a hyena.
He has green eyes like grass.
He goes to Morrisons.
He's the only person that likes Dungeon Keeper.
He's my fabulous best friend ever.

*Simon Parsons (10)*
*Stivichall Primary School*

## The Double-Headed Snake

The double-headed snake was very vicious.
        He had really sharp teeth.
He was very colourful.
        If you ever saw it, he would
Catch you and bite you.
        He would bite you so hard that
You would die.

        If he was alive now there
Would be flames everywhere.
        The streets would be flooded
With rubbish.
        They would destroy the
Whole city.

The snake belonged to a very poor
        Man called Viellavan but
He was a very fierce man, he was evil.
        He didn't like anybody at all.

        *Just Beware!*

**Sophie Meakin  (9)**
**Stivichall Primary School**


## The Temple

It was very hot and still.
The sun beat down on the temple.
The colours of the stone were
Silver, gold and green,
Red, pink and blue.
They were all starting to twinkle in the light.

**Hannah Woodcock  (9)**
**Stivichall Primary School**

## THE SNAKE

What's that smell?
It smells like sweat and slime.
It's coming from that cave over there.
I take three steps up to the cave
And two steps in and
*'Argh'* I say
These bright red eyes stare at me,
A monster with two heads comes steaming out the cave.
I quickly run for my life all huffing, puffing and panting.
'Can't stop now,'
I come to a dead end,
The snake chasing after me,
Next thing I know . . .
He's got me curled up tight.
I can't b-b-breathe.
*'Ahh'*, his mouth goes snap
And there I am in the snake's gruesome gut.

*Samantha Bolus (9)*
*Stivichall Primary School*


## THE TEMPLE

Today a temple is being built,
They have been here for over a year now.
I can see them building the walls,
First it was the earth and stones . . .
Tomorrow . . . it will be used for sacrifices.
People say that one of the ghosts
haunts the town every 100 years.

*Gemma Brown (9)*
*Stivichall Primary School*

## THE TWO HEADED SNAKE

There is a snake with two heads,
he lives down in the earth.
He has a poisonous mosaic gleaming back,
no one dares go near it because
they know it will be arms and legs for tea.
The strange thing about it is sometimes
it's stone and sometimes it's not.
The only way you know it's coming
is when you hear the clanging of the mosaic stones
so beware, beware, of the
snake . . . *argh* . . .

*Chomp, chomp, chomp.*

***Elliot Batchelor (10)***
***Stivichall Primary School***


## AN AZTEC'S MASK

An Aztec's mask, what a sight!
Real teeth and human skull.
Mostly used during the night by the gruesome king
He'll hunt and prowl through the jungle reeds
Turquoise, blue, lignite black,
What a really gruesome sight.
All different kinds of mosaic and gold.

***Jamie Reinwalt (10)***
***Stivichall Primary School***

## The Snake

The snake is large,
The snake is tall,
The snake has two heads,
As huge as your body and as big as mine.
I think you're wondering why it has heads on either side.
I'll tell you now, the reason is quite plain to see,
The reason
Oh, the reason is to . . .
Scare you and me.
Oh no, it's coming to life, I'd better
Run, you'll see,
It's big and thick and squirmy
It's squirming after me.
It has just a few teeth, only a few is true
Although it's fierce and frightening
Me to death.
Ahhh . . .

*Hannah Greyson-Gaito (9)*
*Stivichall Primary School*


## The Temple

The temple was quiet, the sun was rising, and birds were singing.
When the clock struck ten all the people from villages
came in and sacrificed all that was horrible
Then after all of that, everyone went home.
At the end of the day there I lay all alone on my own,
In the dark night with the moon shining.
Then in the morning the same happened over and over again.

*Suneil Jaspal (10)*
*Stivichall Primary School*

## THE DOUBLE-HEADED SNAKE

In the darkness of the night,
There is a snake that gives you a fright.
Its burning eyes make you hot,
It makes you scream a lot.
It's got two heads, they're very big,
It'll eat you up if you're playing tig.
Then it can go underground,
And under there it doesn't make a sound.
*Ssshhh!*
It knows where you are,
So you better run far,
So . . . be careful!
*Aagh!*

**Matthew Mullen (9)**
**Stivichall Primary School**


## SACRIFICE

I'm going to be a sacrifice.
I wish they hadn't picked me.
Sad and scared that's how I feel,
But I know that God will give me a good after-life.
I'm terrified, lying down and waiting, waiting to be sacrificed.
The priest is walking into the temple.
My heart is beating fast, faster than ever before.
Just waiting for that moment.
I can see a sword in front of my face and then everything goes black!

**Lauren Byrne (10)**
**Stivichall Primary School**

## The Snake

The snake's
Gigantic and tall,
With two heads
As large as yours or mine,
Although they look terribly awful and fierce.
You may wonder why these
Ferocious heads are on
Either side of the slimy
Sweaty body?
I think it's to scare us all
And keep us awake at night,
Tossing and turning till morning arrives.

*Kirstie Simpson (9)*
*Stivichall Primary School*


## The Temple

The sun rose, shining bright
the temple was so tall, so beautiful,
birds singing, but when it's sunrise
thousands of people come.
Sacrifice takes place,
the screaming of people having their hearts torn out,
people praying,
but when sunset come it's back to the start.
I sit by myself in the middle of the night
with the moon shining down on me.

*Sam Strumidlo (9)*
*Stivichall Primary School*

## THE MASK

In a deep dark cave
A mask lay still on the sand.
A mask with shining teeth
And a face made out of little stones.
Its eyes are hard marble, global green.
If you leaned forward to smell
You would probably faint
Because of his mouldy skull
And his smelly shining teeth.
His nose is made out of little pieces of bone.
If he came alive you would be a goner
In one second because of his sharp smelly teeth.

*Tom Price (10)*
*Stivichall Primary School*


## THE TEMPLE

The temple was big
And shining gold and silver.
It was shining so much
It looked like it was all made of jewels.
The door opened,
Stairs began to appear,
A priest stood on the bottom step,
He held a knife.
He pointed to me and said
*Sacrifice!*

*Ketna Mistry (9)*
*Stivichall Primary School*

## The Scream

There is a snake far away,
It has burning eyes and it eats its prey.
With its long slithery back,
It secretly slides along the tarmac.
It has two heads so it can eat a multi-pack
Of ice-creams? No, humans to be exact.
It can go underground and under there it can't make a sound.
But only at the black of night does it decide to give you a fright.
It does this because it knows that you'll be more frightened
In the night than in day when all is bright.
It definitely knows where you are so please be careful . . .

*Kimberley Jones (9)*
*Stivichall Primary School*


## Aztec Sacrifices

The sacrifice was quiet and solemn.
When the victim came in to be killed
there was no violence
just silence.
He lay down on the table,
he knew he wouldn't be able to go back
if he did he would upset the gods so he just lay there still.
The priest came with the knife.
His life was slipping out of his hands like sand.
Boom, he was gone.

*Jessica McGarry (10)*
*Stivichall Primary School*

## THE MASK

In a museum far, far away
There was a mask made out of human skull
And his face was covered in stone.
Marble eyes and long sharp teeth,
Sharp enough to kill a man.
It smells so horrid, it could kill you in one single sniff.
If it comes to life it will hop around.
You can't kill it,
It will never die.
So run away, don't tell anyone
Come back next year and it will be gone.

*Ryan Waite (10)*
*Stivichall Primary School*


## RED

The burning of a fire
lighting up the ground.

The colour of the leaves
in autumn, that are
lying on the ground.

The veins in my eyes
that show the anger
that I feel.

The colour of two summer fruits
that taste divine with cream.

And finally the colour of my favourite
football team.

*Elliot Krauze (9)*
*Stratford Preparatory School*

# I Should Like To...

I should like to sleep on the wing,
Just like the swift,
So that I can soar in the wind.

I should like to roll in the waves,
Just like a seal,
So that I can rock to sleep.

I should like to sleep on the hoof,
Just like a horse,
So that I can smell the lovely grass.

I should like to sleep upside down,
Just like a bat,
So that I can look down on the ground.

I should like to sleep underwater,
Just like a fish,
So that I can see their wonderful world.

But best of all I should like to be,
Snuggle up tight,
Turn out the light,
With my bear,
In my own bed.

*Abigail Tompkins (9)*
*Stratford Preparatory School*


# Autumn

Goodbye summer days,
No more sun or fun.
Back to school we go,
The holidays are done.

Hello autumn days,
Red, yellow, russet, gold.
Find acorns and conkers,
Now it's getting cold.

*Charles Hewitt (9)*
*Stratford Preparatory School*

## I SHOULD LIKE TO . . .

I should like to feel the moaning of the corn in the breeze,
The morning dew that scuttles by,
I should like to touch the first breath of a newborn lamb,
And the pond that is so dry,
Everywhere I'd like to feel the clouds above fluffy and white in the sunlit sky,
I should like to point the wind its right direction, to go east, south or north.

I should like to smell the life of Jesus,
God and the Holy Spirit three in one,
I should like to do everything impossible for pleasure like
My mouth smelling,
My ears talking to yours,
My nose feeling the stars,
My hands seeing the song of a blue tit,
And my eyes tasting the wind,
Just for the luxury of doing so forever more.

*Emma Hogg (10)*
*Stratford Preparatory School*

# I Should Like To

I should like to hear
the soaring of a bird,
the whizzing of my brain
as I think.

I should like to taste
the morning's rising sun,
to smell the dancing fairies,
playing in the breeze.

I should like to feel,
the soul of me and you,
an angel up in heaven,
from behind the heavenly gates.

I should like to see
sound travel so fast,
the odour of a skunk
passing by.

*Kelly Gregg (10)*
*Stratford Preparatory School*


# Purple

It's the colour of the evening fire blades,
And the colour of the evening sky.
It's my favourite colour and also my worst lesson.

I think of it as a pigeon flying towards me,
And children throwing snowballs at the kitchen door.
Half the colour of the Christmas tree
It's the colour of an eagle's nest.

*Clementine Hutsby (10)*
*Stratford Preparatory School*

## I Should Like To . . .

I should like to touch
a bird's sweetest song
and hear the flap
of their fluttering wings.

I should like to paint
the wind and
taste the candyfloss
like clouds.

I should like to fly
with the birds,
talk to the moon
and sleep in a soft cloud.

I should like to walk
on water
and ride a whale
around the world.

*Hannah Pashley (10)*
*Stratford Preparatory School*


## Autumn Days

Hello autumn days,
Hello mist and dew,
Russet leaves and conkers,
The sky is misty too.
Jack Frost is in the fields,
Grass twinkles in the sun,
Birds seeking succulent berries,
The summer days are done.

*Rupert Daffern (9)*
*Stratford Preparatory School*

# I Should Like To . . .

I should like to
shoot into space and
look at the Earth below,
from the rocket window.

I should like to hear
the sound of boiling red,
gases, and paint the burning
sun.

I should like to taste
the cheese on the planet
Moon and smell the burnt
dust of exploding stars.

I should like to float
about in the dark timeless
cosmos, and never grow old.

*Olivia Newton (10)*
*Stratford Preparatory School*

## Purple

The strength of a dragon,
The whistle of the wind,
A soft winter morning,
And the sound of the bird warbling

All these things are dark and obscure,
Rough rocks,
Deep seas,
And a lot more.

*Edward Hogg (10)*
*Stratford Preparatory School*

## Yellow

The blazing fire awaits me,
The flashing of the lightning too,
And seeing the middles of daisies
Makes me remember,
Remember the colour I first saw.

The heat of the rays,
The bright sunny months,
The beach in the sun,
Makes me remember,
Remember the colour I first saw.

The sunflowers grow,
The petals shine in the sun,
The stripe on my cardigan,
Makes me remember,
Remember the colour I first saw.

*Emma Hunt (10)*
*Stratford Preparatory School*


## Autumn

Farewell to summer,
Goodbye to the sun.
We will miss the sea and sand,
And all the summer fun.

Hello to autumn,
Hello mist and dew.
Russet leaves and conkers,
We hope we find a few.

*Kate Wells (9)*
*Stratford Preparatory School*

## I Should Like To . . .

I should like to hear
the clouds passing by
and to smell the rain.
I should like to hear
the flowers growing and
to feel the air,
to taste the whistling
of the wind!

I should like to touch
the voice of the birds
as they flitter through the sky,
I should like to smell
the world go by
to play in a picture!
and to soar through the sky!

*Sarah Harris (9)*
*Stratford Preparatory School*


## I Should Like To . . .

I should like to . . .
Feel the sky,
Run away with the sun,
Play with the rain,
And eat the moon.

I should like to . . .
Surf the stars,
Play with Saturn,
Ride the Milky Way,
Fly around the world in a cardboard box,
And see the aliens on Mars,
I should meet the man in the moon.

***Edward Collins (9)***
***Stratford Preparatory School***

## I SHOULD LIKE TO . . .

I should like to paint
the taste of the morning wind,
or the feel of the blackbird's song
and other strange things.

I should like to paint
the flower tasting its food,
or the touch of the still air
and different things like that.

Wouldn't it be strange
if I could paint
the wise old oak tree eating
its morning meal?

***Ross McDermott (9)***
***Stratford Preparatory School***

## THE MONTHS

January's snow is a soft blanket.
February is windy and wet.
March, full of wind and showers.
April sprouts pretty flowers.
In May the birds shout and sing.
The rose, June's flower, is the king.
July brings out the scorching sun.
In August children have such fun.
The harvest starts in ripe September.
Down the leaves fall in rough October.
In November, north winds blow.
December brings soft white snow.

*Sophie Roberts (9)*
*Stratford Preparatory School*


## I SHOULD LIKE TO . . .

I should like to taste a star
To feel it tingling on my tongue.
I want to touch a planet
To feel its shape.
I wish I could see the air
Its gentle movement swaying.
I should like to smell the moon
Does it really smell like cheese?
I want to hear the sun rising
Crackling and yawning awake.
I wish I was a spirit
Then I could do these things.

*Jaryd Buggins (10)*
*Stratford Preparatory School*

## A Place In My Heart
*(Dedicated to my parents)*

In my heart they hold a place,
A place where there is love and joy.
I feel happy that they are with each other,
I feel sad now they have gone.
My life feels so empty.
The two most important people in my life are no more.
My family, friends and even my teachers
Are so supportive and encouraging.
I would have been lost without them.
I miss the way my mother would cuddle me
Every time I got upset.
I miss my mother's happy, cheerful face
After returning from school.
I miss the way my father called me 'Mum'
Every time he saw me.
I felt very close to my mother and father.
I felt that I could confide in my mother
As if she were my friend.
And yes,
I suppose that I feel anger and confusion
That God has taken both of my parents
In the space of a year.
But I also feel happy
As they have been reunited in heaven.
It has put my mind and heart at ease.
I know that I can't bring them both back,
But their thoughts and memories
Shall remain in my heart forever.

*Nishath Hussain (11)*
*The Croft School*

## I'M GOING HAYWIRE!

I'm going haywire today!
I broke my mum's tyre today!
For breakfast I had pliers today
Because I'm going haywire!

I'm going haywire today!
I'm not going to school today!
Although the teacher's cool today
Because I'm going haywire!

I'm going haywire today!
I'm driving up the wall today!
I've a feeling I might fall today
Because I'm going haywire!

I'm calming down today
Because I've had enough today!
I really feel quite rough today!
Being haywire is too tough today!
So I'm calming down today.

*Phew!*

*Eleanor Collins (9)*
*Tysoe CE Primary School*


## I'M GOING FISHING TODAY

I'm going fishing today,
At Shipston river to catch some fish
That are inside the river with my rods,
And the sheep are baa-ing
And the cows are mooing
In and amongst the trees the birds sing.

*Stuart Prickett (9)*
*Tysoe CE Primary School*

## MY STORMY LIFE

My life is like a stormy sea
        That goes on and on and on
It never ends just keeps on going
        Till the tide comes in.
Last year seven ships were sailing
        Along the Seven Seas
One man shouted loudly
        'Man overboard'
Which I of course had done.
        I reached up into my mind
And grabbed the sailor
        So I threw him overboard
For he was bad and mean
        To me, he was my worst enemy.
In real life, the sailor always
        Gets away so I put up
                With it.

*Rachael Nilsson (9)*
*Tysoe CE Primary School*


## EARTH AND MARS

When I go up into my room,
I stare out of my window,
It feels as if I am
Sad and alone,
So I look at the stars,
And all my favourite places,
Earth and Mars.

*Rhian Melton (10)*
*Tysoe CE Primary School*

## THE BLUE CARPET

Bluebells are growing,
I've seen four,
Bluebells are growing,
The sun will be here soon,
Laid out like a carpet,
Oh, how happy I am,
Summer's here soon,
There in the forest,
There in the wood,
There in the garden,
Bluebells are pretty,
Bluebells are sweet,
Bluebells are my favourite flower,
Bluebells are a carpet,
Of a beautiful sight.

*Corrin Ascott (8)*
*Tysoe CE Primary School*


## I LOVE STARS

Stars are hot,
Small and gold,
If I was an alien I would live on a star.
They are yellow and look like balls,
I feel I am walking on a star.
There are so many that they look like money.
There are thousands and thousands like a Milky Way
They make pictures like horses.
I feel like I am flying in space,
That's why I like stars.

*Ashley Guest (9)*
*Tysoe CE Primary School*

## MY BLACK HAIRY FRIEND

I've caught a black hairy spider,
It's tickling me like mad.
It's crawling up my arm now
It wants to be my lad.

It's climbed up to my shoulder,
It's walking everywhere,
It's starting to eat my hair now,
But I'm taking lots of care.

It's fallen down my back now,
It's fallen on my bed,
It's fallen on the floor now . . .

Squelch, it's dead!

*Emily Sayer (8)*
*Tysoe CE Primary School*


## WATERMELONS AND TIGERS

Watermelons and tigers go very well together,
but personally I hate watermelons,
but tigers are something else.
Especially mountain tigers, they are furry, soft warm fuzzy,
Snowy white and dangerous black.
One day I would like to roll down a hill
With a tiger.
But that's in my dreams.
Now watermelons are
Cold and hard, I don't like them.

*Nancy Day (8)*
*Tysoe CE Primary School*

## WOODLOUSE AT SCHOOL

Did you hear about the grey woodlouse?
This is what happened.
We were on the carpet when . . .
'There was a woodlouse on your desk, Miss.'
'Now it's up your skirt, Miss.'
'Now it's through the door, Miss.'
'It's crawling down the loo, Miss.'
'Now he's done a poo, Miss.'
'Now he's out of the loo, Miss'
Then, squelch, squash, he's dead.
What a shame.
Are you afraid of woodlice?
I'm not.

*Jessica Sayer (8)*
*Tysoe CE Primary School*


## THE LLAMA WHO THOUGHT HE WAS AN IGUANA

There was a llama
Who was called Rama
He ate a banana
And thought he was an iguana.
So he married a llama
And got calmer
But the llama was an iguana.
The iguana said 'You stupid llama
You're a banana'
'No you dodo' said Rama
'And you look like a cow' said iguana
And then he ate the llama.

*Gareth Cotter (8)*
*Tysoe CE Primary School*

## UNDER THE APPLE TREE

I lie under the apple tree
Watching the world go by
Listening to the singing birds
Tweeting in the sky
Right above my head they fly
Above the apple tree.

Bugs crawl on the ground
Up my back they crawl now
Right up to my shoulder
Bye, bye spiders on my back
Mum is cooking cookies and cakes
Bye, I'm in for lunch.

*Katie Luckett (8)*
*Tysoe CE Primary School*


## THREE CHEERS FOR MRS BUTLER

*Please Mrs Butler this boy Derek Drew . . .*

| | |
|---|---|
| Keeps *A*ttacking my | *B*udgie Miss. |
| Keeps *C*hasing my | *D*og Miss. |
| Keeps *E*ating my | *F*ruit cake Miss. |
| Keeps *G*iggling at my | *H*airstyle Miss. |
| Keeps *I*rritating my | *J*aguar Miss. |
| Keeps *K*icking my | *L*eft foot Miss. |
| Keeps *M*ummifying my | *N*anny Miss. |
| Keeps *O*perating on my | *P*arrot Miss. |
| Keeps *Q*uacking at my | *R*abbit Miss. |
| Keeps *S*aying my | *T*ortoise will die Miss. |
| Keeps *U*ndoing my | *V*iolet laces Miss. |
| Keeps *W*orrying about my | *X*-ray Miss. |

*Nicola Davison (10)*
*Wellesbourne Primary School*

## In My Magical Alphabet Soup I Would Put...

A ppetising acrobatic astonishing apples.
B ushy bowling balistic bananas.
C razy crunchy crispy carrots.
D isgusting doughnuts.
E normous exciting Easter eggs.
F at frozen fish fingers.
G igantic green gobstoppers.
H airy helping ham.
I cy intelligent ice-cream.
J uggling jealous jam.
K icking karate kiwi.
L azy lying lemons.
M outhy munchy mousse.
N aughty nuts.
O pened oranges.
P erfect popped pickled peas.
Q uick Quavers.
R acing rumbling radish.
S trange sizzling sausages.
T angy tasty tomatoes.
U gly used orang-utan.
V ile vegetables.
W aggling waffles.
E X traordinary X-ray tablets.
Y ummy Yo-Yos.
Z ig-zag zebra.

*Toni Dobson (10)*
*Wellesbourne Primary School*

### IN MY MAGICAL ALPHABET SOUP I WOULD PUT...

A stonishing apples.
B ig blaring bananas.
C orresponding cabbage.
D ifferent doughnuts.
E normous Easter eggs.
F erocious flying figs.
G reat green grapes
H opping handy horseradish.
I cy ice-cream.
J umping jacket potato.
K icking Kit-Kat.
L uscious large lollies.
M agical munchy macaroni.
N aughty navy noodles.
O pen orange oranges.
P ersonal pink paracetomal.
Q uiet Quavers.
R emarkable Ritz crackers.
S melly saucy sandwiches.
T angy Tango.
U ncle Ben's rice.
V aluable Vice Versas.
W atery wrinkled water melon.

*Roxanne Cooknell (10)*
*Wellesbourne Primary School*


### ABOUT YOU

Your head is as round as a football.
Your eyes are like balls of fire.
Your nose is like a big red cherry.
Your hair is as slimy as seaweed.

*Jade Brain (10)*
*Wellesbourne Primary School*

## SIMILES

Your head is as oval as a pineapple.
Your eyes are as big and as red as a tomato.
Your nose is as pointed as a pyramid.
Your hair is as thin, as thin as a bit of straw.

*Adam Payne (10)*
*Wellesbourne Primary School*


## SIMILES

Your head is as oval as an American football.
Your eyes are as round as a tennis ball.
Your nose is as spotty as a Dalmatian.
Your hair is as curly as spaghetti.

*Adam Trinder (10)*
*Wellesbourne Primary School*


## SIMILES

Your head is like a big pink flower.
Your eyes are like sparkling sea water.
Your nose is as pointed as a mountain.
Your hair is as straight as pencil lead.

*Emily Woods (10)*
*Wellesbourne Primary School*

## SIMILES

Your head is like a sparkling apple.
Your eyes are as round as footballs.
Your nose is as slopping as ski-jump.
Your hair is as spiky as a hedgehog's spikes.

*Tom Essex (10)*
*Wellesbourne Primary School*


## SIMILES

Your head is as round as an egg.
Your eyes are as small as a golf ball.
Your nose is as pointed as a mountain peak.
Your hair is as thin as spaghetti.

*Ben Elliott (10)*
*Wellesbourne Primary School*


## YOUR FACE

Your head is as oval as a bell without a base.
Your eyes are hazel, like inside a tree.
Your nose is as wide as a ruler's width.
Your mouth is as crinkly as a crinkled leaf.
Your dimples are as deep as the middle of decayed teeth.

*Lindsey Marie Fullwood (9)*
*Wellesbourne Primary School*

## SIMILES

Your head is like an oval shape.
Your eyes are like Winnie the Pooh's.
Your nose is like a paint patch.
Your hair is as straight as a book.
Your mouth is like a wriggly worm.

*Charlotte Schofield (10)*
*Wellesbourne Primary School*


## YOU

Your head is as round as a circle.
Your eyes are like the blue sea.
Your nose is like a hill.
Your hair is like a yellow river
flowing down a hill.

*Carrie Alford (9)*
*Wellesbourne Primary School*


## ACROSTIC POEM

L aura loves lollipops.
A ngela is my cousin.
U ncle John is funny.
R aspberry picking is fun.
A unty Sue is kind.

*Laura McEveney (9)*
*Wellesbourne Primary School*

## SIMILES

My eyes are like great big footballs.
My nose is like a big orange triangle.
My hair is like a little snake.
My head is as big as a car.
My lips are like lines.

*Chris Waddoups (9)*
*Wellesbourne Primary School*


## SIMILE

Your head is like a round pink ball.
Your eyes are like round shining gold pounds.
Your nose is like the pointed peak of a mountain.
Your hair is like wriggling writhing slippery snakes' babies.
Your eyebrows are as furry and fluffy as a bear's furry frizzy hair.
Your eyelashes are like spiky bee stingers.

*Elizabeth Kyriakopoulou (10)*
*Wellesbourne Primary School*


## BONFIRE NIGHT

Children gathering things for the bonfire.
Now the bonfire has been lit.
The flower fireworks going up in the sky.
The rockets whooshing up, up, up, *bang!*
The flames are going up.
The Catherine wheels are screaming,
Spinning round and round.

*Daniel Kettle (8)*
*Wellesbourne Primary School*

## SIMILES

Your head is as oval as an American football
left there in the middle of the pitch.

Your eyes are as round as a globe
not rotating a single bit.

Your nose is like an orange segment
just about to be eaten by someone.

Your hair is as prickly as a hedgehog's
spikes when he is curled up in a ball.

Your ears are as big as peanuts
still in their shell.

Your cheeks are as rosy as red apples.

Your lips are as exquisite as a lady's nightgown.

*Chris Brindle (10)*
*Wellesbourne Primary School*


## OCTOBER ACROSTIC

O pen the conkers.
C rinkle crackle goes the combine.
T iny animals going to sleep.
O utside in the rain.
B aking conkers ready to play.
E veryone waiting for Christmas Day.
R adiators on everywhere.

*Callam Green (8)*
*Wellesbourne Primary School*

## SIMILES

Your head is as oval as a
squashed ball of plasticine.

Your eyes are like beaming car lights
flashing on the road.

Your nose is as silky and smooth
as a round attractive shell.

Your hair is as thin as
a pointy, spiky knitting needle.

*Graham Shone (10)*
*Wellesbourne Primary School*


## OCTOBER

O wls hoot at night.
C onker shells are ready to break through.
T umbling leaves falling down.
O utside it is raining.
B erries are ready for the birds.
E veryone is happy.
R ain is tapping on the windows.

*Louise Fawcett (8)*
*Wellesbourne Primary School*

## UNTITLED

Ashleigh's always acting.
Sometimes I shout at my friends.
Hair all about.
Love licking lollies.
Eat everything my mum gives me.
I eat ice-cream.
Gift from dad.
Hair's up for school.

*Ashleigh Piotrowski (9)*
*Wellesbourne Primary School*


## SIMILES

Your head is like an American football.
Your eyes are like white ping pong balls,
with little black dots in the middle.
Your nose is like a corner of a book.
Your hair is like curly wurly writhing spaghetti.
Your ears are as big as leaves.
Your eyebrows are as fluffy as a rabbit's tail.
Your eyelashes are as long as my pointed pencil.

*Kylee Smith (10)*
*Wellesbourne Primary School*

## OCTOBER

O range autumn leaves.
C onkers ready to break free.
T umbling, tossing leaves.
O utside is turning cold.
B arn owls are making their homes cosy.
E verybody is busy.
R abbits are getting ready for winter.

*Sophie Tilley (7)*
*Wellesbourne Primary School*


## THE AZTEC DEATH

I saw it, it was the most beautiful city ever built,
Gigantic temples, clean swept streets, statues' faces on a tilt.
Golden temples cleaned every day,
Other tribes with tribute to pay.
Suddenly spears surged towards us - Spanish platoon all captured!
They knocked us round savagely and I struggled with leg fractured.
We were put at the foot of a sky-scraping temple leading up to heaven,
Causeways connecting to *Tenochtitclan* as big as the river Severn.
I knew the devilish creatures were going to kill and eat me,
I was just about to see how my death would be.
It was my turn to serve the gods,
They were going to *eat me!* Like they do to dogs.
I shouted *help me!* but no one could understand,
Because I was so far from the mainland.
They pulled me onto the stone flat,
I could not understand the priest's chat.
He thrust his knife into my chest,
After that I could not rest.
He took my soul,
And hung me on a pole.

*Amardeep S Thandi (11)*
*Whitley Abbey Primary School*

## FOOTBALL'S FUN, FOOTBALL'S FREAKY

Football's fun, football's freaky
You have to run and your eyes get streaky
The goalie's here, the keeper's there
Is he the bloke without the hair?
The defender's coming, the striker's flat
To the defender he's like a rat!
The midfielder's running with the ball
Through the defence just like at school!
The striker's forward in his role
He chips the keeper and it's a *G-O-A-L!*
The fans are chanting, the score's one-nil
The opposition manager looks quite ill!
The chairman groans at the back
He tells the manager 'You've got the sack!'

*Steven Woodward (11)*
*Whitley Abbey Primary School*


## ANACONDA

Agile silent not often seen.
All are afraid of this massive huge giant snake.
Here comes a victim.
Out jumps the giant.
Victim!
Never seen again.
Snake!
Gone down until another day.

*Martin Hawkes (11)*
*Whitley Abbey Primary School*

## LESSONS

The clock strikes eleven.
The handle's pushed.
Everyone's in with a roar
sitting down in class
waiting for the terrible task.
*Maths!*
With a fear
of the teachers.
Pupils sit and stare.
Some don't care so they tear jumpers under the table
wishing to listen to cable.
The bell goes for dinner,
then with a flash the children dash!

*Tara McEnery (11)*
*Whitley Abbey Primary School*


## SNAKES

S nakes, slowly, slither for prey, they hide and *jump*
   out and eat them all in one from top to tail,
N ot all snakes are slow they are
A lso very fast, there are venomous snakes that cannot be
K ept as pets because if they bite there isn't
   a medicine to cure, not
E very snake has venom but most do,
S o you better watch out or you could be next
   to be eaten from top to tail.

*Donna Ann Thacker (10)*
*Whitley Abbey Primary School*

## Up And Around Space

When I stare up and around space,
I wonder what's on that moon face.
Star bugs twinkling high and bright,
Making sure they're in good sight.
Rockets circling the starry sky,
Round and round they will fly.
Satellites photographing,
All the planets orbiting.
So here I sit still wondering,
All that really is happening.

*Esther Sewell (11)*
*Whitley Abbey Primary School*

## Simply The Best

I swam with a dolphin my dream had come true.
What a beautiful creature a lovely colour of blue.
It took me around not once but twice.
The pool was freezing as cold as ice.
The dolphins would swim side by side,
Swimming around giving me a great ride.
It happened in Cyprus, what a lovely place.
The dolphins were gentle and had a beautiful face.
It's time to get out now and let the dolphins rest.
Dolphins are simply, simply the best.

*Karly Jayne Bedding (11)*
*Whitley Abbey Primary School*

## LATER!

My friends all called for me yesterday
As well as today,
Can I play out Mother?
Not yet she would say.

When can I play out then Mother?
Not yet I've just said
And if you keep on pestering me
You won't play out and you'll go straight up to bed.

By the time it was half-past three
I'd have to make the tea
Then at half-past four
Finish the chores before half-past six.

When can I play out Mother?
Not yet I said
And if you keep on pestering me
You won't play out and you'll go straight up to bed.

So by the time I could play out
It was time for bed anyway
There's always tomorrow my dear she'd say
'Cause tomorrow's another day.

***Gemma Louise (11)***
***Whitley Abbey Primary School***

## FREDDY THE DOG AND THE TRAGIC CAT CHASE

The dog called Freddy,
was a marvellous mutt,
who scared the cat out of its body.
But he was as dumb as a sheep.

As the cat runs,
the race now starts
and the dog is ready to kill.
The terrible enemy cat will be obliterated.

But the cat speeds
and the dog barks,
the cat jumps over the wall
energetically over the lake, waiting for an explanation.

The dog speeds,
the dog jumps.
Unidentified flying dog!
But, Freddy, wait, *no!*

*Wooooooofffff!*

The lake,
just horrific silence.
No evidence of Freddy
So ends the life of Freddy, the devilish, ferocious, dumb dog.

*Kirsty Browett (11)*
*Whitley Abbey Primary School*

### STAR-GAZING

At night
I sit
and watch
and look
ready and waiting for the first star
to appear. The moon comes out
the wolf howls and the ghost
rises and then it's here, the
first star of the night, but
then at about one million miles
an hour it shot out of
nowhere. It was not a
star but a UFO. Yes a
UFO. Red, blue, green, white,
black, pink, all the colours
of the rainbow and all you
can think of. Now there
are 5, no 10, no 20, good God
there are lots! Now there are four lasers
coming out. It has pulled up an
old lady, a tree, a cat, four houses. This
will be on the news and it happened
in Coventry in Whitley, this is really
fun. Well not for the old lady, the cat,
and the four houses, and at the speed
of light it has gone and the sky is
dark and
once
again
it's
lonely.

*Nicola J Clark (10)*
*Whitley Abbey Primary School*